Instructor's Resource Manual with Test Bank

The World of Words
Vocabulary for College Students
Sixth Edition

Margaret Ann Richek
Northeastern Illinois University

HOUGHTON MIFFLIN COMPANY   Boston   New York

Senior Sponsoring Editor: Lisa Kimball
Development Editor: Kellie Cardone
Editorial Assistants: Peter Mooney and Sarah Cleary
Manufacturing Coordinator: Carrie Wagner
Senior Marketing Manager: Annamarie Rice

Printed in the U.S.A.

ISBN: 0-618-43290-6

123456789-MV-08   07   06   05   04

Contents

Preface

This *Instructor's Resource Manual with Test Bank* is a supplement designed to accompany *The World of Words: Vocabulary for College Students,* Sixth Edition. Included are notes and comments on each chapter, tests with answer keys, and supplementary exercises with answer keys.

The notes and comments first give general teaching suggestions and activities. This is followed by specific suggestions to accompany each chapter.

The next section of the *Instructor's Resource Manual* provides tests. Each of the first twelve mastery tests covers one chapter; the second set of twenty-four tests contains the same material, but each test covers only half a chapter. There are six review tests provided for Chapters 1 through 4, Chapters 5 through 8, Chapters 9 through 12, Chapters 1 through 6, Chapters 7 through 12, and the entire book.

The supplementary and review exercises—in three formats—are intended to provide students with more contextual practice in using the vocabulary words. Each exercise relates to half a chapter of the text. Multiple-choice sentences are intended for lower-level students. These sentences teach students how to use contextual clues in choosing the best option out of three to complete a sentence. The passage exercises provide higher-level students with practice at inserting vocabulary words and their derivatives into stories. These are relatively difficult exercises involving extensive use of contextual clues. Finally, three sets of review exercises are given: for Chapters 1 through 6, Chapters 7 through 12, and the entire book.

PART I: TEACHING WITH *THE WORLD OF WORDS*

Resources for Teaching

In addition to the **student book** for *The World of Words,* there are three other resources for teaching. (1) The **Instructor's Annotated Edition** contains answers to exercises. (2) The **Instructor's Resource Manual with Test Bank,** which you are now reading, contains suggestions for teaching, tests with answer keys, and supplementary exercises with an answer key. (3) A **Student Website** contains supplementary exercises.

To obtain these resources, call Faculty Services at 800-733-1717, ext. 4015, or fax your request to 1-800-733-1810. The student website may be accessed at http://college.hmco.com/devenglish/students/ dev_reading.html.

Philosophy and Purposes of Text

The World of Words, Sixth Edition, is designed to teach independent learning strategies in a systematic way, to encourage a continuing interest in words, and to develop mastery of a specific set of useful words. Each chapter presents a number of words to be mastered, teaches a learning strategy (dictionary use, context clues, or word elements), and presents interesting features about words.

Mastering Words

Consistent student reaction over several years has convinced me that students want to master specific words in a vocabulary course or in the vocabulary component of a reading or English course. This word learning gives them a sense of concrete accomplishment. In addition, the words serve as vehicles for learning independent strategies, for becoming interested in language, and for understanding the world around them.

These words are presented in the two Words to Learn sections of each chapter. Treatment is detailed enough to encourage in-depth mastery. Often several illustrative sentences or a usage note is given. In the Sixth Edition, special attention has been paid to usage, including connotations and collocations. This is reflected in example sentences, "common phrases," and notes on words. Words are fully defined; if a word has two common meanings, both are given so that students will not be confused when they meet the word in different contexts.

The word list and its treatment grew from several years of experience at Northeastern Illinois University with students of many different backgrounds and reading levels. Three years of piloting and use enabled me to refine the list and to keep only the words that students found most useful. Fifteen additional years of using the first five editions inspired the changes included in the Sixth Edition. The number of definitions, depth of word treatment, and accompanying notes have all benefited from student feedback.

The Words to Learn sections are designed to spark student interest rather than simply to be a dull list of definitions. Hence, the reader will notice lively example sentences and frequently interspersed boxes that expand on common associations of words or present their unique histories.

Review sections following each set of four chapters help students to consolidate their word mastery.

Learning Strategies

Each chapter contains a portion devoted to teaching independent learning strategies. These are integrated with the words in the chapter.

The three strategies presented, dictionary use, context clues, and the use of word elements (or morphology), are precisely those identified in a seminal research review (Baumann, Kame'euni, and Ash, 2002) as critical to vocabulary learning.

Dictionary use   Since most developmental students are familiar but not proficient with a dictionary, Chapter 1 is devoted to efficient dictionary use. Additional dictionary exercises are given in Chapters 3, 5, 7, 9, and 11. Examples and instruction are based on the *American Heritage® College Dictionary,* Fourth Edition (2002). In addition, a pronunciation guide is found inside the front cover of *The World of Words.*

Context clues   Context clues follow in Chapters 2 through 4. They are easily paired with dictionary use and are fundamental to independent vocabulary learning. The three context strategies presented (clues of substitution, definition, and opposition) are the ones students find easiest and most natural to use.

Word elements   Greek and Latin word elements are often found in college-level words and form an indispensable tool for independent vocabulary learning. Therefore, two-thirds of the book, Chapters 5 through 12, is devoted to the study of word elements. Exercises combining the use of context clues with word elements are included in each chapter to ensure that students integrate and internalize their learnings.

The word elements that have been included occur in a number of high-level English words and were selected through a survey of college textbooks. The results of this survey were refined using several published studies and student feedback.

The study of word elements has many advantages for college students. It provides an excellent way of determining the meaning of many higher-level words, particularly those in specialized fields. The use of such words requires a type of higher-level thinking and generalization that improves reasoning skills and reading comprehension, as well as vocabulary. Finally, because most word elements are drawn from Latin and ancient Greek, a study of such word elements gives an opportunity to acquaint students with these civilizations and their many valuable contributions to our present culture. This discussion fascinates my students and helps broaden their background knowledge.

In addition, the Related Words allow students to use suffixes to master the different parts of speech that one word forms. This type of morphology has been increasingly recognized as powerful (Nagy and Scott, 2000). Care has been taken in this book to ensure thorough learning of word elements and the ability to apply them in unknown words. First, the instruction in the Introduction to Part Two and in Chapters 5 and 6 has been carefully sequenced. The Introduction describes prefixes, roots, and suffixes and shows students that word elements often present figurative meanings of words. For example, the word *reject,* which according to word elements would mean "to throw back," has a different meaning in English; students are then shown how to use the literal meaning of "to throw back" as a clue to the current English meaning of *reject.* Following the Introduction, prefixes are treated first and explained through familiar examples. Chapter 5 concentrates entirely upon prefixes. Chapter 6 introduces word roots.

Construction of Word Lists

Extensive checks of word frequency were done using full-text searches of the *Chicago Tribune* and LexisNexis Academic. These rich data bases enabled me to determine word frequency in contemporary usage. Full-text data base searches were refined with statistical findings from studies such as the *Educator's Word Frequency Guide* (Zeno et al., 1995). Findings from all of these sources have helped to refine the word list and words to learn for the Sixth Edition.

The words presented are, on average, at the twelfth-grade level (known by 50 percent or more of high school seniors). I have found that these words are unknown, or only very indistinctly known, by developmental freshman and sophomore college students. My teaching experience suggests that students who do not speak English as a native language can also profit from learning these words.

A second provision to encourage word element learning is the use of a unifying theme for the word elements in each chapter. Chapter 7, for example, presents the theme of "movement"; Chapter 8 presents the theme of "together and apart." These themes encourage more coherent learning by helping students to connect words.

Third, word elements are presented in a way that helps students recognize and use them in modern English words. Students are not given a detailed discussion of precise classical infinitive forms, past participles, present participles, and stems. Rather, they are shown the word-element spellings most frequently seen in English words. More detailed etymological information is, however, given in the "Notes and Comments on Each Chapter," on pages 15–31.

Student Interest and Background

This book is based on the premise that vocabulary learning must be interesting; if students are motivated, learning will be lasting. It is my contention that vocabulary must be integrated into background experiences for words to be fully learned (Richek, 1988). Hence, this book contains features that link student knowledge to vocabulary learning and that cover such subjects as naming customs, car names, and sports headlines. Students enjoy these features and start to see vocabulary learning as an activity that is relevant to their everyday lives. While reinforcing these links, the book also seeks to supply more sophisticated background information. Thus, as the book progresses, information is provided on ancient Greek and Roman culture, famous figures in literature, classic works of art, and scientific advances. All Related Words exercises now contain useful information in paragraph form. Many are continuous treatments of one subject, which allow for more in-depth development. Finally, a Passage in each chapter provides an interesting or informative essay that shows the chapter's words in extended contextual use.

Our college population is increasingly cosmopolitan. Because of this, several features in this book stress contributions to English from other languages, information about other cultures, and links between Spanish and English. The teacher will also note that a wide variety of names has been used throughout the text.

Geographical knowledge is key to information about the world. For this reason, several maps included in the Sixth Edition illuminate concepts discussed in the text. In addition, a world map given on the very first page of the book makes it more truly the *"World" of Words*.

Finally, students must connect to new words by using them in speech and writing. To this end, two exercises require students to use new words in ways that are relevant to their lives. In other words, this book is intended to broaden students' backgrounds as well as to teach vocabulary words and strategies. Research over several years has substantiated the importance of vocabulary in adult IQ (Stahl, 1999; Weschler, 1981) and reading comprehension (Botzum, 1951; Daneman, 1991; Davis, 1944, 1968; Thorndike, 1973). Vocabulary is also an important component in the ACT and the verbal portion of the SAT, both significant predictors of college success (Aleamoni and Oboler, 1978; Houston, 1980; Malloch and Michael, 1981; Mathiasen, 1984; Weitzman, 1982). Many researchers postulate that vocabulary can be correlated with college success because words are the representatives of concepts and knowledge (Adams and Collins, 1979; Lesgold and Perfetti, 1978; Spiro, 1980). Thus, to teach vocabulary effectively, background and concepts must be connected to words. Placing words in such context provides enrichment for the student, makes words easier to learn, and facilitates the extension of vocabulary learning beyond the classroom. Research suggests knowledge is stored in organized schemata in the mind (Spiro, 1980). To be learned thoroughly, the subject at hand must be connected to one's life and experience (Readence, Bean, and Baldwin, 1998). *The World of Words,* Sixth Edition provides a natural and interesting way to make such connections while enriching the student's fund of knowledge.

Ensuring Effective Vocabulary Learning

Recent research in vocabulary learning has shown the importance of two different activities for vocabulary growth. First, a meta-analysis of many studies (Stahl and Fairbanks, 1986) as well as extensive reviews of research (Beck and McKeown, 1991; Baumann, Kame'euni, and Ash, 2002) show that direct instruction of vocabulary has a substantial positive effect on vocabulary growth. Well-formed definitions and examples facilitate the learning of word meanings (Nist and Olejnik, 1995). *The World of Words* provides helpful direct instruction in vocabulary.

In addition, research indicates that students learn a certain number of words incidentally, simply through reading (Jenkins, Stein, and Wysocki, 1984; Nagy, Anderson, and Herman, 1987; Beck and McKeown, 1991). West, Stanovich, and Mitchell (1993) have found that reading is a particularly rich source of vocabulary growth and world knowledge. Thus it is important to encourage students to read as much material as possible. Suggestions for encouraging reading are given on pp. 9–14.

Listening has also been shown to be an effective method for vocabulary growth (Stahl, Richek, and Vandiver, 1991). Suggestions for using this mode are also included.

Organizing Instruction

Student Level Appropriate for Book

Results of a three-year pilot study and fifteen years of using the text at Northeastern Illinois University show that this book may be used successfully with students reading from the seventh-grade to the eleventh-grade level. In addition, some students reading at even lower grade levels have used it; those students have had to work hard, but they have succeeded. The book has also been used by students reading at the twelfth-grade level or at college levels.

The book is appropriate for students from many different backgrounds. The student population at Northeastern Illinois University is cosmopolitan, and the book has been used by students from more than fifty different language backgrounds. It has proven eminently suitable for those whose native language is not English. Features on such topics as the Dalai Lama, Jackie Robinson, Samuel Maverick, and words borrowed from other languages in English ensure wide and varied student appeal.

Planning the Course

The World of Words can be used as a basic text in a vocabulary course or as a supplementary text in a reading, study skills, or English course. I suggest that it be used at the rate of one chapter per week or half a chapter per week. If used in half-chapter segments, each chapter might be divided as follows:

First week
    Quiz Yourself
    Did You Know?
    Learning Strategy
    Words to Learn, Part 1
    Exercises, Part 1
    Mastery Test from the **test bank** for first part of chapter

Second week
    Words to Learn, Part 2
    Exercises, Part 2
    Chapter Exercises
    Passage
    Making Connections
    English Idioms
    Mastery Test from the **test bank** for second part of chapter

This organization encourages consistent learning by breaking up the coverage of the Learning Strategy over two weeks. In the first week, the strategy is introduced and reinforced by the words; in the second week, the Chapter Exercises reinforce the strategy.

Some instructors may not wish to give chapter or half-chapter Mastery Tests but would prefer to test several chapters at one time. They can simply use the Review Tests, each of which covers four, six, or twelve chapters.

Each four-chapter Review Test (Chapters 1 through 4, 5 through 8, and 9 through 12) contains twenty-five items. Like the Chapter Mastery Tests, each is divided into a matching segment and a sentence-completion segment. The matching segments for Chapters 5 through 8 and 9 through 12 do not, however, include word elements.

Each six-chapter Review Test (Chapters 1 through 6 and 7 through 12) contains thirty-three items. Thirteen of these items cover learning strategies (including word elements), and twenty cover vocabulary words.

The Review Test for the entire book contains fifty items. Seventeen items cover the learning strategies (including word elements), and thirty-three cover vocabulary. This test may be used as a final.

If time demands in the course allow, I strongly recommend that students use the Review Exercises provided in the student text and in the supplementary exercises of this manual. These exercises help consolidate learning. Students may feel apprehensive about reviewing a hundred or so words (one wise guy in my class cried out, "Hey, I thought this was an *easy* course!"), but they also appreciate the time to rest and review. Each Review Test has a set of related exercises. Review Exercises for Chapters 1 through 4, 5 through 8, and 9 through 12 are presented in the student text. Review Exercises for Chapters 1 through 6, Chapters 7 through 12, and the entire book are in the supplementary exercises of this manual.

In my course, which lasts fifteen weeks plus one exam week, students review Chapters 1 through 4 during the fifth week, Chapters 5 through 8 during the tenth week, and Chapters 9 through 12 during the fifteenth week. Exam week contains a review and test of the entire book.

Organizing tests and keeping them confidential With so many tests to give, I have to devise a way to organize them. I've developed a color-coded system, printing the tests in cycles of five colors. The use of colors helps me to sort my tests easily and to find them quickly.

I maintain test security by not allowing students to take tests from the instructional room. I also ask students to clear their desks while taking tests. The colors help me to notice when the occasional test is inadvertently about to be removed. In addition, after I have graded and given back tests for discussion, I collect them again. Only after they are in my permanent possession is the grade recorded. This ensures that students will not keep their tests and circulate them. This system also provides that, in case of a query, I can easily locate the completed tests.

An excellent idea for checking exercises was provided by a fellow instructor, who reviewed the book manuscript. This instructor requires students to complete all exercises, but collects and grades only a few each week. Since students do not know which exercises will be collected, they must complete them all. However, the grading burden is not overwhelming for the instructor.

Chapter Format and Exercises

A consistent format for each chapter encourages systematic student learning:

Quiz Yourself—a true-false pretest on four words.

Did You Know?—a section highlighting an interesting fact about everyday words.

Learning Strategy—a systematic introduction to the use of the dictionary, context clues, or word elements.

Words to Learn—Part 1—twelve words and accompanying exercises.

Words to Learn—Part 2—twelve words and accompanying exercises.

Chapter Exercises—a review of learning strategies, word usage, and a writing exercise using the words that have been learned.

Passage—an informative or inspiring passage using at least fourteen of the chapter's twenty-four words. Knowledge of these words is tested in an accompanying exercise and in discussion questions.

Making Connections—an exercise requiring students to make an extended written (or oral) personal response to three chapter words.

English Idioms—a presentation of several common English idioms, focused around a chapter-related theme.

Numerous and varied exercises in *The World of Words* assure mastery of words and learning strategies. The exercises in the Words to Learn section have these purposes:

1. A matching exercise provides immediate reinforcement of learning by asking students to match a word (or phrase containing a word) to its definition.

2. Words in Context, a sentence-completion exercise that requires students to write out the words, gives practice using words in context.

3. Using Related Words gives students practice with derived forms. A few sentences on a single informative topic contain two to four cloze blanks. The student fills in various forms of a single word to complete the passage. The alternatives are presented (e.g., *exuberance, exuberant)*. In this exercise students are sometimes required to write out the past-tense and third-person-singular forms of verbs as well as noun inflections. This gives them practice in working with forms that are often used incorrectly in writing. Teachers also may wish students to write down the part of speech of each word that they use to fill a blank. The exercise presents continuous discourse (rather than discrete sentences). This provides more contextual reading and gives students additional opportunities to acquire background information. The Sixth Edition increases the amount of informational material in this exercise and, in addition, provides some exercises that form one continuous narrative.

4. Which Should It Be?, True or False?, and Reading the Headlines are application exercises that require students to apply their knowledge to more difficult language. One of these exercises appears for each group of twelve words. These more challenging tasks help students to consolidate their mastery over words.

The Chapter Exercises have the following purposes:

1. Writing with Your Words contains ten "sentence starters" that must be continued by students to form complete sentences. The following items are examples:

   I know a person so *gauche* that _____.

   When I gave my *candid* opinion, _____.

   This exercise gives students an opportunity to practice writing in a controlled situation and to use newly learned words creatively. I find that students express themselves in personal ways that deepen vocabulary learning and camaraderie. Students should be encouraged to write longer phrases and to avoid one-word answers. Some will find this exercise quite challenging and may want to complete it orally rather than in writing. Other students may be encouraged to work in pairs, composing one set of written responses. The creative aspect of this exercise makes it a favorite with my students.

2. Companion Words has students choose the preposition (or other small word) that follows a Word to Learn. This gives students the practice that enables them to use words comfortably.

3. A set of Practicing Strategies exercises in Chapter 1 encourages students to consolidate dictionary skills by interpreting dictionary entries, using a pronunciation key, and doing independent dictionary research. Since dictionary use is a skill that is often learned slowly, additional exercises for reinforcing dictionary skills by interpreting dictionary entries are found in Chapters 3, 5, 7, 9, and 11. *The American Heritage® College Dictionary,* Fourth Edition, is the source of the exercises.

4. The sets of Practicing Strategies exercises in Chapters 2 through 4 encourage students to apply context clues. They must read sentences that contain such clues and then make a hypothesis of a probable meaning for a difficult word. Instructors may integrate dictionary use with this exercise by having students check their answers with the dictionary. A particularly valuable exercise in Chapter 2 has students infer new meanings for common words like *air, stormed,* and *shy.*

5. In Chapters 5 through 12, three exercises reinforce word element learning:
   a. Immediately after the student learns the elements and words that use them, a reinforcing exercise has the student match word elements to their meanings.
   b. In the Chapter Exercises section, students apply their knowledge of word elements by identifying other words formed from these word elements. Using the chapter's word elements, students choose words that are not presented in the chapter and insert them into defining sentences.
   c. In the exercise Combining Context Clues and Word Elements, students read sentences in which one difficult word contains a word element they have been studying. The student then uses both context clues and word elements to work out the meaning of the word. An example is:

      Using the *autofocus* feature of a camera, even an amateur can take a clear picture.

      Autofocus means _____.

6. The Passage in each chapter is accompanied by a short, multiple-choice exercise that checks that students have read the passage and can show an understanding of words in extended contextual use. Three comprehension questions are also included to spark class discussion. One instructor, Joyce Jennings, uses the Passage to *introduce* each chapter. As the Passage is read, students hypothesize the meanings of the chapter words.

7. Finally, new to the Sixth Edition is a Making Connections exercise that presents three questions (or statements) that students must respond to in extended form. This provides an opportunity for more thoughtful, personal responses and for writing practice. Of course, students may be asked to prepare these questions for discussion.

Supplementary Exercises in the *Instructor's Resource Manual*

It has been my experience that students need many opportunities to use a word in context before they can fully understand and use it. Two supplementary sets of exercises are provided in this manual to further aid students.

1. For students at a lower level, there are sets of Multiple-Choice Sentences. Each sentence contains a blank followed by three words from which the student must choose the correct one. This exercise provides easy practice in context and helps students develop strategies for taking multiple-choice tests. The exercise also gives students experience in choosing the *best* of three alternatives. There are twenty-four of these exercises, one for each half-chapter.

2. For more advanced students, twenty-four Passage exercises have been written. Each one is a passage on a single topic and contains ten blanks that students must fill in from twelve alternatives. These include derived forms of chapter words.

Website Exercises

The supplementary exercises in this manual are also available on a student website. To access this website, go to *http://college.hmco.com/devenglish/students/dev_reading.html* and search by title or author.

Review Sections

After each four-chapter segment, a review section is presented in the text. Each of these sections contains several types of exercises.

1. Words in Context, for filling words into sentences.

2. Passage for Word Review, for filling words into a connected passage.

3. Reviewing Learning Strategies, for practice in strategies (dictionary use, using context, and using word elements) that have been covered in the four previous chapters.

Several of the Words in Context and Passage exercises are based on the writing of my students.

Additional Ideas for Fostering Student Learning

Supplementary Reading

In recent years, I have been encouraging students to foster their own vocabulary learning by reading as much as possible on their own. To do this, I ask them to bring in interesting things that they have read. I assure them that such sources as the daily newspaper or *Reader's Digest* are perfectly acceptable. In addition, I require students to read at least one book during the semester.

In one format, each student reads the same book, and we have group discussions as the students finish selected chapters. For several semesters, I assigned Farley Mowat's *Never Cry Wolf* (available in paperback). This book is read during the last five weeks of the class. Several words that have been taught, or that contain word elements that have been taught, are found in *Never Cry Wolf*. A colleague reports that her developmental students have profited from writing individual book reports. More recently I have used the nonfiction book *How to Win Friends and Influence People* by Dale Carnegie. Although not new, the book inspired much discussion and some changes in behavior.

In another collaborative group format, I briefly describe three (or four) books, and students write out their first and second choices. Based on these, I assign the students books to read with small groups. Generally, each book is read by two small groups. Every time they meet, the group discusses the chapters they have read and each member prepares an assigned job. The jobs, which rotate, are:

Discussion Leader and "Hot Spot" Locater
    Lead the discussion, making sure that everyone does his or her job. At the end of the discussion, present at least one spot that was difficult to comprehend.
Vocabulary Finder
    Locate five difficult vocabulary words and determine definitions. Other members in your group will check them with you.
Summarizer and Reactor
    Briefly summarize the article (in two or three sentences) and write a personal reaction.

Books suitable to this collaborative format include *The Water Is Wide* by Conroy, *The Color Purple* by Walker, *Kramer versus Kramer* by Corman, *I Heard the Owl Call My Name* by Craven, *Like Water for Chocolate* by Esquivel, *Dances with Wolves* by Blake, and *Seabiscuit* by Hillenbrand.

Depending on their levels, I also encourage students to take home and read young-adult novels, such as *Pigman* by Zindel, *The Great Gilly Hopkins* by Patterson, *Where the Red Fern Grows* by Rawls, *Roll of Thunder, Hear My Cry* by Taylor, and *The Outsiders* by Hinton. An occasional student has also read children's books such as *Charlotte's Web* by White or *Roosevelt Grady* by Shotwell. Sports biographies are also popular with many of my students. I often just bring a variety of books to class and pass them out to encourage reading.

I have also asked students to read interesting newspaper editorials aloud in class. The practice in oral reading is beneficial, and the class enjoys discussing the editorials. One student has even braved the *New York Times* op-ed page.

One instructor, Phyllis Glorioso, helps students to familiarize themselves with computer-based library searches by giving them a "media assignment." In this, they choose terms such as *family business* or *Russian bilingual education* and find (1) a newspaper article, (2) a popular journal article (such as one from *American Psychologist* or *The Reading Teacher*), and (3) a magazine article (from, say, *Time* or *Business Week*) that deal with this topic. They summarize each article and locate and define at least five words that seem to be used in their chosen field. Finally, each student makes a five- to ten-minute presentation in class, which summarizes what he or she learned and presents and defines the five (or more) chosen words. This assignment sharpens research skills, encourages independent word learning in an area of interest, and builds oral presentation abilities.

Personal Word Cards

Making word cards is one way to encourage systematic study habits in developmental students. Word cards can be constructed from 3" by 5" index cards. The front of the card gives the word and, in the upper right-hand corner, the chapter of the book in which the word was found. The back of the card might have the pronunciation of the word, a definition (formulated by the student), and an example sentence. If the student is ambitious, two sentences might be included, one from the book and one by the student.

Students can quiz themselves or each other on word meanings and pronunciations using these word cards. They can be encouraged to form three piles of words: words well known, words known but needing further work, and unknown words.

Students can also incorporate words found outside of the text into their word cards. If the word comes from another text, the card should contain an abbreviation for the book on the front right-hand corner. If found in general reading, the source should be abbreviated as "G."

Expert Word Cards

In another adaptation of vocabulary cards, Sharon Lansdown (1991) had students share their word learning by each becoming an "expert" in a few of the many words to be learned. I have used this strategy very successfully in my class; I find it encourages enthusiasm, active learning, and a sense of mastery. The words may be taken from a text chapter or from a book that students are reading. If taken from a book, they may be chosen by the students (before reading) or identified by the instructor. In the strategy, each student is responsible for a few words.

To become an "expert," the student constructs a card for the words he or she is assigned. The card is simply a half piece of construction paper, folded over, that opens vertically. On the outside, the student writes the word. Next, the student writes the definition and a sentence on the inside. (Often students need instructor input to make these accurate and interpretable.) Finally, on the outside, below the word, the student draws a picture that serves as a reminder of the word. Thus, the word *crimson* may have a picture in red magic marker of blood running from a wound. To summarize:

Outside of card: Word and picture
Inside of card: Definition and sentence

The students then are paired with partners. Each partner teaches his or her partner the words. After about ten minutes the partners rotate, and each person gets a new partner.

I have had much success with this strategy, which, among other things, allows students to personally and visually interpret words (Readence, Bean, and Baldwin, 1998). My students become active word learners and often ask, "Is class over so soon?" It also fosters the ease and conversational tone that is essential to successful developmental learning. When they leave class, the students deposit their word cards with me, so that I am certain they will be available for the next review.

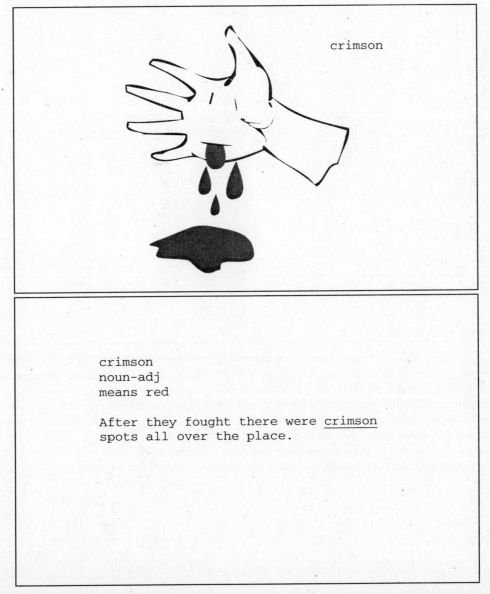

crimson

crimson
noun-adj
means red

After they fought there were <u>crimson</u>
spots all over the place.

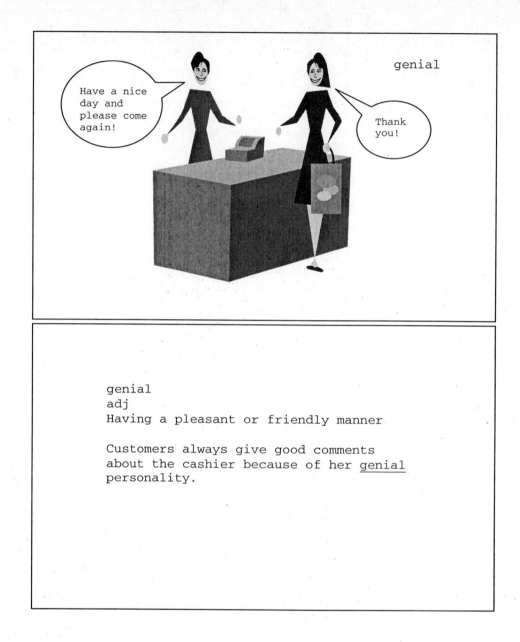

Bringing in Words

I encourage students to bring to class examples of chapter words that they come across in other texts or in general reading. This helps them to integrate vocabulary learning. In addition, when we are studying context clues, I ask students to bring in a paragraph that contains a very difficult word. The student reads the paragraph, highlighting the difficult word, and the class tries to infer the meaning of the word from the context. The magazine or text in which the word was found should also be identified as another clue. The Internet has added a new dimension to this activity. Words are now easier to locate, so examples have multiplied. A colleague who reviewed this book keeps a file of words, collected from encounters in books and newspapers. This provides readily accessible examples when words are discussed.

The Words-in-a-Sentence Game

Like swimming, playing the piano, and pitching on a softball team, vocabulary is a skill that benefits from use. The following game, which I stumbled on accidentally, is guaranteed to involve even the most recalcitrant student. The game takes about twenty minutes for thirty students to play.

Students are separated into permanent teams of three or four people. Each team gives itself a name, which is written on the board. (Names seem to generate considerable enthusiasm.) Then each team takes five words (from the week's work or a list) and writes them on a slip of paper. Each team then gives its list of words to another team.

Once a team has received a list, its job is to use all of the words in as few sentences as possible. Students must write the sentence(s) down. Related words may be used (e.g., *adroitness* for *adroit),* and the teacher may assist with spelling or grammar.

Finally, each team reads its sentence(s) orally. Assuming the words are used correctly in the sentence, the following point system is used:

A sentence with one word—one point

A sentence with two words—three points

A sentence with three words—five points

A sentence with four words—seven points

A sentence with five words—ten points

Thus, if a team produces one sentence with three words (five points) and two sentences with one word (two points), its total is seven points. Of course, the total points are added and compared. The students may wish to keep a running total of points.

This simple game is always received enthusiastically by students. Sometimes even students who have lacked motivation will take the words home and try to get them into one sentence. The instructor may assign one member of the team the task of reading the sentences orally, ensuring that quiet students or students who speak English as a nonnative language receive some oral practice.

The Two-Team Game

This game is excellent for giving continued practice. The class is divided into two permanent teams. The words to be studied are written on slips of paper and put in a paper bag, and then a word is pulled from the bag. A student on one team must pronounce it (for one point), define it (for one point, or two points if there is more than one definition), and use it in a sentence (for one point). If the student can do these three things, the team gets three (or perhaps four) points. A member of the other team then gets a turn. Teams may challenge the pronunciation, definition, or sentence of their opponents.

This game is valuable because it systematically gives each member of the class a chance to participate. It also builds relationships among members of the class: team members with a good mastery of the words often start to tutor members who are experiencing more difficulty.

The Automaticity Game

Beck and McKeown (1984) stress that to be learned well, vocabulary must become automatic. To this end, I have adapted a game they devised with great success. I compose a series of statements to which students must quickly answer "yes" or "no" as a group, or individually by holding up cards. Examples from words in the first chapter might include:

Is an *affluent* person rich?

Does a *stoic* person complain?

Is a *novice* experienced?

I find this game supplies the practice needed to learn words well. In addition, it is fast-paced and enjoyable.

Words in Conversation

Some instructors conduct a conversation once per week on a previously announced topic. During conversation time, require each student to use at least one of the words in the vocabulary chapter being studied.

Listening

I often duplicate difficult but short selections and then read them to my students. Poe's *Cask of Amontillado* and Dickens's *A Christmas Carol* (where Scrooge meets Marley's ghost) are both valuable—and out of copyright. With the former, I challenge students to translate the complex sentences into simple English. We act out the Dickens selection, including sound effects. I have also used excerpts from collections like *Eyewitness to History* (Carey, 1987), which consists of reports of historical events from antiquity to the present. At times, I put difficult words on cards, give each student one or two cards, and ask students to hold up their word when I read it in the selection. This focuses attention on difficult words.

Student-Generated Passages and Journals

I encourage my students to compose passages containing words they have learned in class. In some classes, they get a few "extra credit" points. Fellow students are invited to fill in the cloze blanks. Students have written about the homeless, the fact that the Chicago Cubs needed a mascot, and experiences during the War in Iraq.

In other classes, I require students to write a passage containing five words from Chapters 1–4, 5–8, and 9–12 when they finish these chapters. Students explore various topics in their essays, including their pet cats, their best friends, their used (but beloved) cars, the nicknames they had in high school, and descriptions of native countries. The student essays featured in the review chapters of the book originated from this assignment.

A final suggestion for a writing assignment is to ask students to write about something they have done successfully. Students enjoy this assignment, and have reported on topics ranging from learning English to playing football to making good coffee.

In addition, I might ask students to correspond with me by keeping a journal. Two times per semester, each student writes to me (about anything he or she wishes) and I answer back in the journal. Two students recently told me that this was their first "free writing" experience in English and that it had fostered several other writing activities.

Culminating Assignments

For several semesters, I have required students to do a culminating assignment that uses the words they have learned. They may choose from a variety of options, including writing a passage using ten words, creating a crossword puzzle for fifteen words, highlighting fifty occurrences of learned words in a newspaper, finding or creating pictures to represent ten words (e.g., a picture of a Rolex watch to represent "exorbitant"), and writing poetry or song lyrics. My students enjoy the creativity of this project, which, on the last day of class, they present to their peers.

Notes and Comments on Each Chapter

Introduction to Part One

The Introduction is a guide to the plan of the book and a reference section for future use, covering the parts of speech, the use of inflectional and derivational suffixes, and pronunciation changes. I find that developmental students' lack of knowledge about the parts of speech makes vocabulary books, grammar books, and writing books difficult to comprehend. The explanation in this section gives students a basis for further learning and prepares them for an in-depth discussion of the dictionary in Chapter 1. In addition, it deals with some troublesome usage points (such as the past-tense suffix).

The discussion of suffixes and pronunciation prepares students to work with the Related Words throughout the book. To point out the importance of suffixes, I often have one student choose a passage from a magazine or newspaper to read orally. The other students count the number of suffixes used. Generally, we count six or seven suffixes in each *line* of text.

Chapter 1

Did You Know?

Most students are fascinated and amused by the meanings of their names. Students can try to find their own names in a book such as *Name Your Baby* or at websites like *http://www.babycenter.com* and *http://www.ssa.gov/OACT/babynames/index.html*.

My school has a varied student population, and we cannot always find names such as Su (a Korean name), Minh (a Vietnamese name), or Ahmed (an Arabic and Egyptian name). I ask these students to investigate the meanings of their names, and they usually come up with answers. Students with Spanish names can often use English cognates (such as *Oswaldo/Oswald,* "divinely powerful"). In this context, I usually ask my students to list all the languages that they speak. I often find I have a number who speak two languages, a few who speak three, and an occasional student who speaks four. This activity engenders great respect for the capabilities of students who speak English as a nonnative language.

Hook (1983) finds that names can affect people's perceptions. In a study conducted in California, essays identical in quality were submitted under common names (Michael, David) and uncommon ones (Elmer, Hubert). Teachers graded boys' essays submitted with uncommon names lower than those with common names; for girls, however, there was no grade difference.

Learning Strategy

Although most developmental students have been repeatedly admonished to use the dictionary, few have mastered this tool. The instruction in the text leads them through two entries, a simple one (*amicable*) and a complex one (*rule*). Many students will actually be surprised that there are different types of dictionaries. With this instruction, students should become familiar with the level of detail typical of a college dictionary. Of course, online dictionaries and databases are now common.

My students seem to have considerable difficulty with identifying the number of parts of speech functions in dictionary entries, using the various forms of nouns and verbs (plural form, past-tense form, etc.), and ordering etymologies in a correct (not backwards) fashion. In addition, finding the best definition for a word in context is a perennial problem.

In *The World of Words,* dictionary instruction teaches students how to use a pronunciation key, which is given inside the front cover of the book. To facilitate integration of dictionary use with vocabulary instruction, the book uses the same pronunciation system as the *American Heritage® College Dictionary,* Fourth Edition. A special pronunciation exercise in the Chapter Exercises section helps students to understand this key. You may also wish to have students use the key to pronounce some of the words in the Words to Learn section.

An important dictionary exercise in the Chapter Exercises lets students do some independent work in any college-level or unabridged dictionary. This acquaints them with a more detailed dictionary than the pocket ones they are likely to purchase.

Words to Learn

I find that the format of the Words to Learn section is usually clear to students; however, you might want to explain it. Two changes are new to the Sixth Edition. First, nouns that are persons, such as *novice* and *renegade*, are discussed. Second, the construction in which a noun can be used before another noun as an adjective, such as in *novice driver* and *renegade soldier,* is addressed. For Part 1, students might want to think of *intrepid, hypocritical, ascetic,* or *altruistic* people that they know.

For Part 2, *candid* comes from the Latin verb *candēre,* "to be shining white." This reflects the spotless purity of one who is always truthful. The word *candle* and *candidate* also come from this source. In ancient Rome, a *candidate* for high office suggested his purity by wearing a pure white toga, the color of which had been intensified by rubbing in chalk. Thus the candidate was clothed in "shining whiteness."

Stoic is one of many English words that derives from Greek philosophy. *Epicure,* a person with refined tastes, derives from Epicurus (341–270 B.C.E.), who advised avoiding superstitions and pursuing pleasures. Although Epicurus believed in simple pleasures that led to peace of mind, the meaning of *epicurean* has changed to pursuing the pleasures of the senses. The word *cynic* came from an ancient Greek philosopher who taught in a gymnasium called "Cynosarges," a word that resembled the ancient Greek word for *doglike* (*cynikos*). Thus *cynic* (doglike) was an expression of contempt for this school of philosophy, whose members had little interest in material possessions or cleanliness. *Skeptic,* another word from Greek philosophy, is presented in Chapter 3.

My students enjoy discussing *aliens* that appear in current TV shows and movies.

Passage

In addition to Ben & Jerry's Homemade Inc., other companies have shown altruism, social concern, and concern for the environment. Benetton, a clothing manufacturer, has run ads promoting AIDS awareness, tolerance, and (in conjunction with Amnesty International) awareness of human-rights violations. The proceeds of Phish Food (note the pun) flavor go to environment efforts in Lake Champlain.

Ben & Jerry's flavors often have allusive names. Your students might enjoy discussing associations to *White Russian, Chunky Monkey, Rainforest Crunch* (with Brazil nuts and cashews), and *Chubby Hubby.* Be sure to have your students visit the website *http://www.benjerry.com.* My favorite place is the "Flavor Graveyard."

Idioms

The color (and substance) gold is used in many idioms. Your students might be interested in *golden handshake, golden parachute, gold mine, golden oldie, golden years, golden age,* and *goldbrick.*

Chapter 2

Did You Know?

Sports headlines can be used to teach connotation and the figurative use of language in a colloquial context. In class I usually ask someone to read me that day's sports headlines and to find synonyms for *win* and *lose.* (Somebody always brings the paper to class.) Sometimes I ask students to bring in sports headlines with these synonyms underlined. Here are a few more samples of the several hundred I have collected:

Cold-shooting Loyola falls short

49ers run over Lions

Bills crush Raiders, keep rolling

Bearcats struggle, then cruise

Rocky start, Tee-rrific finish as Tennessee winds up on top

Pitt purrs past Army

Ohio State surprises Rutgers

Learning Strategy

Surprisingly, many students are unfamiliar with the use of context and are very excited to discover this strategy. Clues of substitution are presented first because they seem to be the clues that students use most naturally. Often college students find it difficult even to identify the words they do not know. To help them use context, I ask them to bring in something they have read that contains one unknown word, which they must underline. (I often suggest they use *Reader's Digest.*) I pronounce the word for them in class. Then they read aloud the paragraph that contains the word, and the class must guess the meaning of the word from context. We check this meaning with a college dictionary.

Words to Learn

Every student who has attended college is familiar with the concept of, if not the word, *bureaucracy.* The word *catastrophe* lends itself to a discussion of news events such the 9/11 catastrophe, and the U.S. government response. Do students feel that deportations and limitations on the rights of trial are unwarranted? What do you think is sparking the spate of suicide bombings in Turkey, Iraq, and Sri Lanka? Students can also search the web for natural catastrophes, such as earthquakes, hurricanes, and floods. Finally, *media* is a complex word that deserves discussion.

In Part 2, students enjoy discussing their ideas of the *epitome* of a great football star, a movie star, or evil. A copy of the *National Enquirer* can sometimes be used to locate a *ludicrous* story. Do they agree that Ludacris is ludicrous? Students may also be asked to identify *reactionary, conservative, liberal,* and *radical* politicians. Do they agree that conservatives control the media? Although most students have heard these four words, they often have difficulty using them with precision.

Passage

Sneakers have now achieved almost iconic status in the United States. What other contributions have been popularized by poor, urban areas? What are, for example, some additions to our language (through changed meanings for words, such as *bad*)? You might also discuss whether, in view of the changing role of sneakers, they should be acceptable as formal wear. The book *Where'd You Get Those?* describes the emergence of the shoe through popular culture.

Idioms

In a provocative comment, now-deceased pop artist Andy Warhol predicted that every person would be famous for fifteen minutes. Thus, through media hype, each of us, regardless of merit, could be made, at least briefly, into a celebrity. To underline the fact that people of little talent were being made into celebrities simply by having their name and image repeatedly exposed, Warhol featured unknown actors as "superstars" in his often outrageous movies. The phrase "fifteen minutes of fame" is now widely used. Do your students feel that Warhol was an accurate social commentator?

Chapter 3

Did You Know?

These are some car names you might want to discuss. Students can add the names of their own cars.

Mustang, Pinto (wild horses)

Pontiac (a famous Native American warrior)

Century (a car built to go one hundred miles per hour)

Impala (a fast-running African animal)

Stratus and Cirrus (cloud types)

Aurora (dawn)

Avalon (an island paradise to which legendary King Arthur went after death)

Eagle, Ram, Lynx, Stanza, Sunbird, Citation, Reliant, Tempo, Omni, Sentra, Blazer, Breeze, Lumina, and Avenger

The fascinating history of the automotive industry is a worthy research topic. Early innovators such as Henry M. Leland, Ransom E. Olds, David D. Buick, the Studebakers, and the Dodge brothers both cooperated and fought bitterly as they created a product that revolutionized our lives. Leland, for example, improved the Olds engine, but Olds rejected the improvement. Leland then took the engine to Henry Ford and associates, but Ford quit the gathering, leaving to form the Ford Motor Company. With the remaining participants, Leland invented the Cadillac, which was sold to General Motors in 1908. But, after yet another disagreement, Leland quit GM and organized the Lincoln Motor Company. Leland sold his company to Ford in 1920.

In addition, some of the earliest cars had steam engines and could reverse and go forward with equal speed.

Learning Strategy

The defining context clues are generally straightforward. If students have trouble with appositives, these additional sentences may be used for practice.

Some ants use a *formicary,* an ant's nest.

Druids, members of the ancient Celtic priesthood, once were common in Ireland.

She wore *frangipani,* a red-jasmine perfume.

Students may also enjoy looking in other texts to see how technical words are defined. Texts use all of these devices plus some others, such as printing a word in boldface type or supplying a glossary.

Words to Learn

Enigma is derived from the ancient Greek verb *ainissesthai* (to speak in riddles). There remain many enigmas, which can be discussed in class. For example, several South American cities (including Vaxactun) were mysteriously abandoned over a thousand years ago, apparently at the height of their prosperity. The plain of Nazca, on a Peruvian hillside, contains markings that resemble an airplane landing field. These were built centuries before humans could fly, and some hypothesize that they were intended for aliens.

In Part 2, students may enjoy considering the word *antebellum* in relation to *bellum* (for belligerent). Most students have seen the movie *Gone with the Wind* and remember its depiction of the antebellum South. Was this accurate? Hattie McDaniel, the African American actor who vividly portrayed "Mammy" was not invited to the premier! Her life makes an instructive research project.

Passage

There are stories similar to that of Jackie Robinson's that students may find informative. They can be told about Marian Anderson, the famous contralto who was prohibited from singing at Constitution Hall in 1939 because she was African American. In protest, a group of citizens, including First Lady Eleanor Roosevelt, arranged a concert at Lincoln Memorial that drew 75,000 people. Miss Anderson was the first African American to sing at the Metropolitan Opera in New York.

The fascinating history of African American baseball has been featured in recent years and can be found in such books as William Brashler's *The Story of Negro League Baseball* (1994, Ticknor & Fields) and John B. Holway's *Blackball Stars: Negro League Pioneers* (1988, Meckler). The video set *Baseball: A Film by Ken Burns* (1994) also honors Negro League players. African American baseball brought many distinctive and entertaining contributions to the game. Rube Foster's Chicago American Giants dominated the game in the 1910s and 1920s.

The contributions of African Americans are shown in every field of endeavor. In invention, to give a few examples, Dr. Charles Drew invented a way to preserve blood plasma. Otis Boykin originated the control unit used in pacemakers and many other electronic devices. Frederick Jones gave us the portable X-ray machine and the self-starting gasoline motor. Granville T. Woods initiated the automatic air brake and the telephone receiver. The almost innumerable inventions of George Washington Carver include even peanut butter.

Chapter 4

Did You Know?

The size and international nature of English always fascinates students. Here are some foreign borrowings: *cotton* and *apricot* from Arabic; *yogurt* and *kiosk* from Turkish; *orange* from Arabic, Persian, and Sanskrit. The word *salt* comes from ancient Greek, meaning both "sea" and "salt." The word *salary* (from Latin *salarium,* meaning "salt money") is derived from *salt,* since in ancient Rome workers often received a ration of salt for their work. Looking up the origin of one's favorite food is a painless way to practice dictionary usage.

The New Words Team of the Oxford English Dictionary selected sixty-two words that "offer a fascinating snapshot of the past twelve months." These include *ego-surfing*—searching the Internet for your own name; *uplift anxiety*—a term to describe psychological problems that arise from being cured of depression; *web rage*—(from *road rage*), anger due to slow Internet access; *waitress mom*—a parent of low income; and *microphobes*—opponents of Microsoft Corporation. The comeback of yo-yos has repopularized *walk the dog, milk the cow,* and *reach for the moon* as yo-yo routines.

The *Los Angeles Times* has reported, from business, new words such as *cube farm*—offices made of rows of cubicles, and *to prairie dog*—to pop up over the side of your cubicle when you need a little break and just want to have a look around. Internet coinings include *404*—formerly known as *airhead,* from a "404" web message stating that the document cannot be found. Internet acronyms include FWIW—for what it's worth, and RTM—read the manual.

A few suffixes have done might work in forming new words. In the 1970s, President Richard Nixon resigned over the *Watergate* incident. Since then, the suffix *-gate* has brought us *Camillagate* (Prince Charles' significant other), *Nannygate* (in honor of a murdering nanny), and *Zippergate* (referring to Bill Clinton's behavior). *Alcoholic* has spawned *workaholic, shopaholic,* and *chocoholic.*

The *Atlantic Monthly* sometimes contains a "Word Watch" feature by Anne Soukhanov, former editor of the *American Heritage Dictionary.* In this she discusses new words being considered for dictionary inclusion. Back columns are available on the Internet through *theatlantic.com.*

Learning Strategy

The first two opposing structures are the easiest for students to recognize because they contain words that clearly signal the opposition. The following sentences will provide students with additional practice in recognizing the last two opposing structures.

Sam is complacent and *hardly ever* feels uncertain about his actions.

That typewriter is obsolete and has been *unused* for many years.

Words to Learn

The many senses of *cultivate* are often difficult for students. You might ask them if they know anyone who is cultivated or if they have ever tried to cultivate a friend.

Military jargon is a rich source of euphemisms. These include *friendly fire, neutralize a target* (kill the enemy), and *collateral damage* (the hitting of unintended targets, such as hospitals and schools).

In the clothing industry, "relaxed fit" means pants for overweight people. Even "senior citizens" was coined as a euphemism for the elderly.

Mammoth gets its current meaning of "enormous" from the large size of the extinct mammoth, a hairy type of elephant. *Chivalrous* derives from the Latin word for horse (*caballus*). *Chivalry* was first used to refer to nobles, who were rich enough to afford horses. Later the word came to mean a code of honorable conduct supposedly characterizing the nobility. My class enjoys making lists of other animal words and phrases. One group came up with these:

loan shark	to hound	foxy
sing like a canary	lounge lizard	a wolf
snake in the grass	turkey	to parrot
hogwash	rat	to carp
lionize	catty	old goat
horse around	chicken	

Cryptic derives from the ancient Greek verb *kruptein,* "to hide." Similar words use the concept of hidden in different ways. A *crypt is* an underground hidden chamber, often carrying the meaning of burial place. The cracking of codes or hidden messages is called *cryptanalysis,* and a code breaker is called a *cryptographer. Cryptic coloration* in an animal is used to camouflage, or hide appearance.

Exercises

The Related Words exercises in Chapter 4 present the life stories, in continuous narrative form, of Eleanor of Aquitaine and Elvis Presley.

Passage

My students think this topic is hilarious. Further readings on this topic include *You May Not Tie an Alligator to a Fire Hydrant* by Koon and Powell, and *The Little Book of Loony Laws* by Green. The website *http://www.dumblaws.com* lists laws by state.

Review: Chapters 1–4

Students Rocio and Sophia Ruiz wrote the essay that formed the basis of the "Trouble Twins" sentence exercise. The piece was completed as a class exercise and read to class members. I feel that it speaks with humor, straight from the heart, and shows the high quality of the developmental students I am privileged to teach.

The Names piece gives information that supplements what is presented in Chapter 1 on an endlessly fascinating topic.

Introduction to Part Two

This Introduction establishes the groundwork for the study of word elements by guiding students from the analysis of words that are relatively straightforward (e.g., *impolitely*) to more metaphorical analyses (such as *reject*). Prefixes, roots, and suffixes are distinguished. In addition, roots are divided into base words and combining roots, the latter being more important for the development of higher-level vocabulary skills. Many prefixes and roots will be covered in Chapters 5 through 12. Since most suffixes are derivational (in that they change the part of speech rather than adding lexical meaning), they receive less emphasis. However, lexical suffixes such as *-meter* and *-logy* are included. Remind students that a hyphen after an element indicates a prefix; a hyphen before indicates a suffix. In other words, a hyphen is provided where a base word or combining root would be joined.

Chapter 5

Did You Know?

Since a knowledge of classical cultures is important to an educated person, you might want to spend a few minutes discussing the ancient Greeks and Romans. My students generally enjoy hearing about Plato's *Republic* and the *academy* at which he taught. (This was named for the mythical hero-student Akadēmos. From his name, we also derive *academic.*) The unexpected victory of the small city of Athens over the mighty Persian empire on the plain of Marathon in 490 B.C.E. also interests students. A messenger ran back to Athens to report on the victory, and from that run *marathon* has come to mean "long-distance run." The Romans are remembered for their excellent administrative skills and the oratory of speakers such as Cicero. *Oration* comes from the Latin verb *orāre,* which means "to plead, speak, pray." Our word *senate* comes from the Latin *senatus,* which means "council of elders." *Senex* is Latin for "old man" and *senile* derives from the same source. Those students with some knowledge of the Renaissance should be reminded of the importance of classical studies in that period of history.

The Related Words exercise of this chapter expands on knowledge about the ancient Greeks and Romans.

Learning Strategy

This first lesson in word elements concentrates entirely on prefixes. Each of them is free-forming and can be used with base words. Examples are *antinuclear, equidistant, retry, subcontract, ex-president,* and *invalid.* Caution students, however, that *re-* and *ex-* have two very distinct meanings. Instructors with a background in classical languages will already know that many prefixes were derived from Greek or Latin prepositions. Further etymological information is given below.

Part 1

> *Anti-* comes from a Greek preposition and prefix of the same spelling. The prefix is spelled *ant-* before vowels.

> *Equi-* is from the Latin adjective *aequus,* meaning "equal." The spelling change took place when the word was used in Old French. The prefix is spelled *equ-* before vowels.

> *Re-* is from a Latin prefix of the same spelling.

> *Sub-* is a Latin preposition meaning both "under" and "below."

Part 2

> *Auto-* is from the Greek word for "self," *autos.*

> *In-:* This set of prefixes is complex. The "not" meaning comes from the Latin prefix *in-,* similar to the Germanic prefix *un-.* The other meaning, "in," is from a Latin preposition and prefix *in,* meaning "in, into, toward, against." The spelling *im-* is used before *p, m,* and *b* (these are all labial consonants), as in *impartial, immodest,* and *imbibe. Il-* is used before *l* (*illogical*), and *ir-* is used before *r* (*irrational*). The *ir-* and *il-* spellings always indicate "not."

> *Ex-:* Both Latin and Greek had prepositions, *ex* and *ek,* that meant "out of." When used as prefixes, they changed to *e-, ec-,* or *ef-,* depending on the first letter of the root. Currently, *ec-* is used before *c* (*eccentric*), and *ef-* is used before *f* (*effervescent*).

Words to Learn

It is particularly important to relate each word to its word elements in this lesson. An additional discussion topic for Part 1 might be the accusation that the livestock industries have been feeding animals too many *antibiotics.* (This word is included in a note under *antidote.*) Antibiotics enable the animals to live in suboptimal conditions, making care less expensive, but both the animals and humans (through eating their meat) may be overexposed to such medicines. In addition, strains of bacteria may mutate so that they are not killed off by the antibiotics. Recently, this practice has been thought to be the root of outbreaks of salmonella poisoning. Feeding practices are also thought to contribute to BSE, or Mad Cow Disease. *Equilibrium* comes from the same root as *Libra,* a sign of the zodiac symbolized by balance scales. Libras are said to be even tempered, and thus possess *equilibrium.*

For Part 2, undoubtedly somebody's *autobiography* is now on the best-seller list and can be discussed. The two meanings and pronunciations of *exploit* are difficult for students to distinguish. You might discuss child labor to give a sense of one meaning, and some current adventure stories for the other.

Exercises

The two Related Words exercises in this chapter are each related within their sets. The first gives a continuous, if very abbreviated, narrative of the history of the Roman Empire. This topic will be revisited, with the life history of Julius Caesar, in the Passage of Chapter 9. In the second Related Words exercise all topics center around Ancient Greece. I felt that these topics would enrich students' knowledge of ancient Greece and Rome, and hence enhance the appreciation of the role of their languages in modern English.

Passage

My students enjoyed the topic of SPAM® immensely. A few even volunteered the fact that it was a relative's favorite food. Of course, in the modern world, *spam* has taken on the meaning of unwanted e-mail. A debate currently rages on whether the outlawing of spam would be wise, and whether such a prohibition would violate the First Amendment, which guarantees freedom of expression. On a lighter note, Hormel's SPAM® website, *http://www.spam.com,* is the best I have ever seen. It features outstanding music and seven decades of SPAM® history. Your students can also search the Internet for interesting SPAM® recipes and uses. Note that, like *motel* and *smog, spam* is a portmanteau word.

Chapter 6

Did You Know?

Other words taken from names include: *guy* from Guy Fawkes, who was hanged for conspiring in the English Gunpowder Plot of 1605; *mausoleum,* from Mausolus, a king of Asia Minor whose wife built a beautiful tomb for him; *sadistic* from the Marquis de Sade (1740–1814), whose writings described people who liked to torment those they loved. Similar words that you might want to discuss with all of your students are *gerrymander, laconic, ostracize, sisyphean, vandalize, tantalize, thespian, zinnia, Barcelona, Boolean algebra, Cincinnati, bloomers, America, ampere, Bakelite, batty, bowdlerize, camellia, cardigan, derby, diesel, draconian, Geiger counter, leotard, mesmerize, Morse code, nicotine, pasteurize, Richter scale, saxophone, silhouette,* and *volt.*

Learning Strategy

This important section introduces root words and shows how they are used. Students should be encouraged to read it carefully. Part 1 word elements are all roots; the elements in Part 2 are two prefixes (although both are occasionally also used as roots) that relate to mythical figures. The etymological information follows.

Part 1

>*Anthrop (o):* The word *anthrōpos* meant "human" in ancient Greek. Although sometimes it is given as *anthropo,* many words simply employ *anthrop,* so the latter form is used.

>*Gen:* In Greek, *genos* means "birth, race, kind." In Latin, *gignere* is the verb for "to bring forth," and *genitus* is its past participle.

>*Nom* and *nym:* The Latin word for "name" was *nōmen.* The Greek word was *onoma,* later *onyma.*

>*Viv* and *vit:* In Latin, *vīta* means "life" and *vīvere* is "to live."

Part 2

>*Pan-:* As stated in the text, Pan, the god of woods, delighted all. However, the meaning of *pan* as "all" predates the Greek myth, which merely personifies the word. *Pan* is the neuter form of the Greek *pas* (stem, *pant-*) meaning "all, every."

>*Psych-:* Again, the mythology personified a term, *Psukhē,* later spelled *psychē,* as the ancient Greek term for "breath, spirit, life, soul." The spelling *psycho-* is also used in English.

Words to Learn

Wars seem to spark genocide. Are the students familiar with the genocide attempts directed at Jews and Gypsies (World War II) and the Armenians (World War I)? Would the murders of fellow Cambodians by Pol Pot in the 1970s be considered *genocide?* How about the 1990s "ethnic cleansing" in the Balkans and in Rwanda?

The well-known character Scrooge is used to exemplify a *misanthrope.* For students who wish to explore the world of Charles Dickens further, Epstein's *Being a Good-Natured Guide to the Art and Adventures of the Man Who Invented Scrooge* provides much information. An entire chapter is devoted to Dickens's use of names. Can students think of more *pseudonyms?* Rap and hip-hop artists are a fertile source for this investigation.

The *viv-* words give students a chance to discuss musical terms, most of which are Italian and thus directly descended from Latin. Do students know the meanings of *vivace, moderato, largo, piano, forte?*

Part 2 words should interest students and spark much conversation. Students may know the musical or movie *Man of La Mancha.* Spanish-speaking students are usually familiar with *Don Quixote.* Famous phrases (other than those cited in the text) found in *Don Quixote* include "give the devil his due," "the pot calls the kettle black," and "the pink of courtesy." These and others can be found in books of quotations. The author of *Don Quixote,* Miguel de Cervantes (1547–1616), was the son of a traveling apothecary-surgeon. As a boy he developed a passion for reading. He fought on a Spanish ship against the Turks and was injured. Later, he was captured and taken into slavery in Algiers. He escaped, but was later recaptured, and this escape attempt was followed by another unsuccessful one. Finally the 500 gold ducats needed for his release were raised, and he returned to Spain.

Many English words and expressions come from Homer's *Iliad* and *Odyssey.* These include the expressions *bite the dust* ("fall headlong in the dust and bite the earth") and *eat your heart out.* A *siren* has come to mean a seductive woman. *Mentor,* a trusted counselor of Odysseus, was left in charge of Odysseus's son when the hero left for war. In Odysseus's absence, Mentor advised the hero's wife not to remarry. Finally, in honor of his great strength, *Ajax,* a Greek hero of the *Iliad,* has had a modern-day cleanser named for him.

Exercises

Continuing with an emphasis on ancient Greece, the first Related Words exercise features this civilization. The first four paragraphs are about Greek myths, a topic that will be echoed in the story of Persephone in the chapter Passage.

Passage

The myth of Persephone captures students' imaginations. Have students heard any other myths? Myths can now be explored through the Internet on such sites as *http://www.loggia.com/myth/myth.html* and *http://www.exotique.com/fringe/Mythology.htm.*

Chapter 7

Did You Know?

This section acquaints students with inventions that have names derived from Latin or Greek word elements. I ask students to list other inventions such as the microphone, typewriter, computer, or video recorder, and we then see what word roots they contain. To further emphasize the importance of classical word elements, I often have students note the large number of derivations from classical roots found in modern scientific words. In chemistry, for example, *atom* comes from *a-* (without) and *temnein* (to cut), both from Greek. *Nucleus* means "kernel" in Latin and is derived from *nux* (nut). *Oxygen* comes from word elements meaning "giving birth to acid" in ancient Greek; *hydrogen* means "giving birth to water."

Learning Strategy

The word elements in this chapter all deal with movement. This theme facilitates student concept formation but also can cause some confusion. Words formed from these word elements require imaginative, metaphorical thinking. The following are the etymologies of the word elements.

Part 1

>*Duct* comes from Latin *ducere,* meaning "to lead" (past participle, *ductus).*

>*Ject* from Latin *jacere,* meaning "to throw," also appears as *jactus* (past participle) and *-jectus* (past participle of the form combining with prefixes).

>*Stans* and *stat* are from the Latin and Greek verbs *stāre* and *histasthai* (to stand). *Stans* is the Latin present participle form; *statos* means "standing" or "placed" in ancient Greek.

>*Ten* and *tain* are from the Latin verb *tenēre* (to hold), with the past participle *tentus.* The *tain* form (in *contain, obtain*) reveals an ancestry through Old French, in which a spelling change took place.

Part 2

>*Tract* is from the Latin verb *trahere* (to draw, pull) and its past participle *tractus.* The spelling in *distraught* reveals a Middle English change.

>*Vers* and *vert* come from the Latin verb *vertere* (to turn) and its past participle *versus.*

>*Circum-* is from the Latin preposition and prefix of the same spelling, meaning "around." *Circus* means "circle."

>*Trans-* is from the Latin preposition and prefix of the same spelling, meaning "across, over, beyond, through."

Words to Learn

Perhaps because of the abstractness of the word elements or the similarity of the words, I often find that students confuse many of the words in this chapter. For this reason, you might want to devote additional time to the words in Chapter 7.

With their several meanings, *deduction* and *abstain* are particularly hard to master. Students often enjoy discussing Sherlock Holmes and his many *deductions.* I also discuss different religious holidays—Lent, Ramadan, Yom Kippur—that require *abstinence.* Some scientists now consider the following theory *tenable* although not proven, of course. Once every twenty-six million years, a star called Nemesis comes close to the Earth and sprays it with destructive meteorites. The extinction of the dinosaurs may be linked to the passing of Nemesis, or another celestial body, near the Earth.

In Part 2, the concept of *perverse* may need some explanation. Some students may have perverse brothers, sisters, or children, who do exactly the opposite of what they are told even if it harms them. Several public officials are *circumspect,* but others are not. You might discuss current scandals of people who did not demonstrate this characteristic. *Circumvent, circumscribe,* and *circumspect* are particularly confusable, and must be practiced.

Passage

Students find the analysis of body language amusing and informative. I demonstrate some poses or let a willing student try a few. With a good-humored class, common postures of students and the instructor might be discussed.

Chapter 8

Did You Know?

The fusion of Old French and Old English is a topic of great interest to speakers of all Romance languages. Since many of my Romance-language-speaking students speak Spanish, I often follow up by having them use an English or Spanish dictionary to list fifty English-Spanish cognates (a small fraction of the total). This topic also helps students to see why speaking a language other than English can help one's English. Of course, Romance languages did not make the only contribution to English (although theirs is the largest). The words *pajamas, bungalow, thug, punch* (the drink), and *shawl* all come from the languages of India and Pakistan. Authors have also contributed to the growth of English. Among the words first recorded in Shakespeare are *cater, cold-blooded, discontent, hurry, lonely,* and *puke.*

Learning Strategy

The theme of together-and-apart concentrates on prefixes in Part 1 and roots in Part 2.

Part 1

Com-: From the Latin preposition and prefix *cum,* meaning "with," this prefix has many variations: *col-* (joined to *l*), *com-* (joined to the labials *p, m,* and *b*), *con-,* and *cor-* (joined to *r*).

Dis-, from the Latin prefix of the same spelling meaning "apart," often means "not" in current usage.

Syn- is from the Greek preposition *sun* (which became *syn* in Latin), meaning "together, alike." Variants are *syl-* (before *l*), *sys-* (before *s*), and *sym-* (before labials *b, p,* and *m*).

Part 2

Greg: The Latin *grex,* with the stem *greg-,* means "flock of sheep, herd of cattle."

Spers is from the Latin verb *spargere* (to scatter, distribute). Other forms include *sparsus* (past participle) and *-spersus* (combining form of the past participle).

Words to Learn

For Part 1, students may enjoy discussing some of the *communes* that were formed during the 1960s. The word *contemporary* should be stressed in both its senses. Students like to discuss whether their parents have contemporary values, as well as the contemporaries of their parents. (Older students often discuss their children in these same contexts.) How many *synthetic* fibers can students name? A few are *rayon, nylon, polyester.* Can they name any natural fibers? *Syndromes* such as *carpal tunnel, autism, toxic shock, Gulf War,* and *attention deficit disorder* are often in the news. Can students think of others?

In Part 2, students might want to spend a few days listening for clichés and reporting the ones that are most common. This is particularly profitable for students who do not speak English as a native language.

Passage

The inspiring story of the role of the Navajos in World War II is now becoming well known. The History Channel, a part of A & E Television Networks, published an excellent 50-minute video titled *Navajo Code Talkers.* It is available through New Video Group, 126 Fifth Avenue, NY, NY 10011. In addition, the Choctaw Code Talkers, who operated in both world wars in the European theater, received recognition only in 1986. Similarly, seventeen Comanche men operated in the European theater in World War II. Among their codes was "crazy white man" for Hitler and "pregnant airplane" for bomber. Both nations were honored in 1989, when France bestowed its highest national honor on the heroes, naming them Chevaliers de l'Ordre National du Mérite.

Review: Chapters 5–8

Two review exercises are based upon the writings of students in my fall 1998 class. Both are stories of triumph over adversity. First, student Viem Nguyen tells of his difficult escape from his native Vietnam in the late 1980s. Then, William Mojica relates how he overcame shyness and slight stature to become a champion runner, only to be brought down by injuries. Viem is now working in computer programming; William is serving in Afghanistan.

Chapter 9

Did You Know?

This section gives further background knowledge on the Romans and may interest students in everyday words. You might like to discuss the origins of the days of the week. *Sunday* and *Monday* are Old English translations of the Latin "day of the sun" and "day of the moon," respectively. *Tuesday* through *Friday* have Germanic origins. *Tuesday* means "day of Tiu," who was the god of war and sky. *Wednesday* means "day of Woden," who was the chief god. *Thursday* means "day of Thor," who was the god of thunder. *Friday* means "day of Freya," the goddess of beauty. Finally, *Saturday* comes from the Latin for "day of Saturn." Originally all the days of the week were named after Latin gods, but some were changed to honor Germanic (often Norse) gods. Latin derivatives for days of the week can be seen in the French *lundi* and Spanish *martes*. Bilingual students can list them and relate them to the Roman gods introduced in Chapters 5 and 6.

Learning Strategy

Twelve word elements are given for numbers and quantities. Since many follow a pattern, my students find them relatively easy to learn.

Part 1

   Uni- is from Latin *ūnus* (one).

   Mono- is from ancient Greek *monos* (alone, single).

   Bi- is from Latin *bis* (twice).

   Di- and *du-* are from *dis,* meaning "twice" in ancient Greek, and *duo,* meaning "two" in Latin and ancient Greek.

   Tri- is from ancient Greek *treis* and Latin *trēs,* both meaning "three."

   Dec- is from ancient Greek *deka* and Latin *decem,* both meaning "ten."

Part 2

   Cent- comes from Latin *centum,* meaning "hundred."

   Ambi- and *amphi-* derive from Latin *ambi* and ancient Greek *amphi,* both meaning "both."

   Ann- is from Latin *annus,* meaning "year."

   Integer- is from the Latin adjective of the same spelling, meaning "whole, entire."

   Magn- and *mega-* derive from Latin *magnus* and ancient Greek *megas,* meaning "large."

   Meter is from ancient Greek *metron* (measure).

Words to Learn

In Part 1, students might be asked to think of *dilemmas* that have confronted them. For *monarch,* the word element *arch* (leader, ruler) might be discussed in relation to such words as *archenemy, archbishop,* and *matriarch.* The word *anarchy* will be learned in Chapter 11.

In Part *2, ambivalent* might be discussed. Perhaps some students have had ambivalent feelings toward a course that was difficult but valuable, or they may have ambivalent feelings about other people. The students might be able to think of athletes who have exhibited *magnanimous* behavior in victory and others who were not so gracious. What would a magnanimous victor say? They can also look for *symmetrical* objects.

One Using Related Words exercise gives a brief biography of Julius Caesar and thus relates to the Passage on Cleopatra.

Passage

Perennially fascinating, students find it hard to believe that Cleopatra was not beautiful. Was she a seductress? A power-hungry manipulator? The record is unclear and sparks lively discussions in my class. Cleopatra's goat milk baths get a resounding YUCK! However, Lucknow University in India recently received a process patent to investigate the medicinal qualities of goat's milk, which might play a role in treating AIDS.

Chapter 10

Did You Know? and Idioms

Idioms using animal words are so plentiful that a number can be given just for birds. These include *featherweight, a feather in one's cap, featherbedding, ruffled feathers, soar like an eagle, talk turkey, stool pigeon, to sing like a canary, goosebumps, silly goose, mother hen, bill and coo,* and *as the crow flies.* Can students think of more?

Learning Strategy

The word elements in this chapter center on faith and belief. The etymological information follows.

Part 1

Cred comes from the Latin verb *crēdere,* meaning "to believe"; its past participle is *creditus.*

Fid is from the Latin *fidēs,* meaning "faith."

Ver is from *vērus,* the Latin adjective "true," and *vērum,* the Latin noun for "truth."

-Phobia comes from the Greek word *phobos* (fear, terror).

Part 2

De-: The Latin preposition of the same spelling means "down from" or "away from." As a prefix in English, the meanings of *de-* include a pejorative sense, which occurs in *delude,* one of the chapter words.

Non- is from the Latin *nōn,* meaning "not."

Words to Learn

The modern sense of *credit,* derived from the Latin sense of belief, might be discussed. Students are always interested in *phobias.* Phobos, the Greek deity personifying fear and terror, was often painted on shields to frighten enemies. Here are a few more phobias to inspire students: *glossophobia,* fear of speaking in public; *ochlophobia,* fear of crowds; *triskaidekaphobia,* fear of the number thirteen (note the derivation from Greek *three* and *ten*).

In Part 2, students might enjoy learning about the Old *Deluder* Satan Bill of 1647. This was the first comprehensive act for public education, passed in Massachusetts. The strict Protestants felt that unless children could read the Bible, they would be deluded by Satan: ". . . it being one chief project of that ould deluder Satan to keep men from the knowledge of the Scriptures." Therefore, they mandated education. The term *nonchalant* might be related to the figure of speech "hot under the collar."

The figures of speech are particularly valuable to students who speak English as a nonnative language. *Star-crossed* makes reference to astrology. Do your students read their horoscopes?

You might want to supplement the figures of speech presented by mentioning *left-handed compliment, play a trump card, red-letter day,* and *between the devil and the deep blue sea.* Some of these have interesting histories, which students may want to explore.

The website *http://www.facstaff.bucknell.edu/rbeard/diction.html* now contains an excellent etymological phrase dictionary that includes origins.

Passage

Superstitions fascinate all of us, and many people feel just a little uncomfortable sitting in the thirteenth row of an airplane. The origins of superstitions about thirteen and Friday can be found in the Christian religion. Jesus and his twelve disciples formed a group of thirteen. Judas, who is said to have betrayed Jesus, was perhaps the first unlucky thirteenth. Many people will not seat thirteen people around a table in an unconscious reminder of the Last Supper. Similarly, Friday was the day Christ was crucified. My students often ask me whether certain superstitions are true. One wanted to know whether, if you dream you are dying, you will actually die.

In this context, you may hesitate to recommend websites, but there are many to be found. An excellent book on follies, many of which served as the bases of passages for previous editions, is Charles Mackay's *Extraordinary Popular Delusions and the Madness of Crowds* (1841; 1980, Crown Publishers).

Chapter 11

Did You Know?

Students may think of other vivid junk food names such as *Twinkies* and *Jolt.* On the other hand, other food names, including *Lite, Fiber One,* and *Total,* suggest health. An excellent book on the history of junk food and food in general is Carolyn Wyman's *I'm a Spam Fan* (1993, Longmeadow Press).

Learning Strategy

These word elements deal with the body and health. The etymological information follows.

Part 1

Audi: The Latin verb *audīre* (to hear) has the past participle *audītus.*

Patho and -*pathy* come from ancient Greek *pathos,* meaning "suffering."

Ped: The Latin *pēs,* with the stem *ped-* means "foot."

Spec comes from the Latin *specere,* meaning "to look" (past participle, *spectus*).

Part 2

A-: The Greek prefix *a-* means "not," with the particular sense of "without." The *an-* variant is used before vowels.

Bene- is from the Latin verb *bene* (well).

Bio- and *bio* come from ancient Greek *bios* (life).

Mal- is from the Latin adverb *male* (ill, badly).

Words to Learn

The importance of *pedigrees* in former times often amuses students. Until the twentieth century, nobles often ordered elaborate studies of their ancestries. Since members of the nobility commonly married each other, most were related. Students can be asked to identify the family ancestry of the late Diana, Princess of Wales. Pedigrees are still very important in the breeding of racehorses.

In Part 2, the students might consider the relationship of *biopsy, benign,* and *pathologist* in relation to the diagnosis of cancer. You might also discuss the word *malignant.* Do students feel there should be limits to *malpractice* suits?

Passage

The story of Jenner's smallpox vaccination is one of the great triumphs of medical science. Many vaccinations for diseases have been developed to protect against polio, whooping cough, tetanus, measles, and (recently) chicken pox. Nevertheless, diseases remain, such as AIDS and ebola, which can be neither prevented nor cured.

Idioms

Other idioms containing food include:

in a pickle	apple of my eye	use your noodle
drive me nuts	act like a nut	say "cheese"
egghead	nuts about you	cut the mustard
butter me up	top banana	you don't know beans
take the cake	cool as a cucumber	alphabet soup
you're a honey	clam up	peachy keen
bread (money)	peachy	cheesecake
juicy story	wet noodle	spill the beans
got a beef	dough (money)	corny
hot dog	something's fishy	out to lunch
macaroni (fashionable)	a meaty issue	

Chapter 12

Did You Know?

Other clipped words include *e-mail, mob* (from Latin *mobile vulgus,* "unstable crowd"), *fan* (from *fanatic*), *flu* (from *influenza*), and *piano* (from *pianoforte*). Acronyms include A.M. and P.M. (ante and post meridian), C.E. (of the common era) and B.C.E. (before the common era).

Learning Strategy

Although word elements comprise an important part of this lesson, the confusable word pairs are also important. Etymological information for the word elements follows. *Dict, log,* and *voc* can be confusing, so warn students to study them carefully. They do not have as much difficulty with *graph* and *script.*

Part 1

Dict is from the Latin verb *dīcere* (to say). The *dict* spelling is derived from the past participle *dictus.*

Voc comes from the Latin noun *vōx,* meaning "voice"; its stem is *voc-.* The Latin verb *vocāre* (to call) and its past participle, *vocātus,* are other sources of words with the roots *voc* and *vok.*

Loq comes from the Latin verb *loquī* and its past participle *locūtus,* meaning "to speak." The ancient Greek word *logos,* meaning "word, speech," gives the *log* and *-logy* forms.

Part 2

>*Graph* had its source in the Greek verb *graphein,* meaning "to write," and the related words *graphos* (written) and *gramma* (letter).

>*Scrib* and *script* come from the Latin verb *scrībere,* meaning "to write," and its past participle, *scriptus.*

Words to Learn

For Part 1, students may discuss recent events related to *ecology,* since this is a subject of continuing interest in the news.

In Part 2, students may want to know that the word *paragraph,* containing the word element *graph,* originally meant "beside *(para)* the writing." A paragraph was a mark made by the side of writing to show that a topic or speaker had changed. Students might cogitate over the meaning of the epigram "Man proposes, God disposes" found in an exercise in the chapter. The confusable words are very important for correct writing. For extra practice, students might try filling word pairs into these frames:

affect, effect

The _____ of the snowstorm was to paralyze the city.

The snowstorm had a terrible _____ on the city.

The snowstorm will never _____ the city.

The _____ of the snowstorm will not _____ the election.

conscience, conscious

My _____ would never let me do that.

I am not _____ of a desire to steal.

A good _____ is valuable.

I am _____ that my _____ guides me.

imply, infer

By your actions, you _____ that you are pleased.

We _____ from your actions that you are pleased.

I would never_____ such a thing in my speech.

If you _____ things, people will _____ them.

Passage

The story of Hedy Lamarr illustrates the many facets of this intriguing woman. Sadly, her life did not develop well. At one point she was destitute, and was even accused of shoplifting! Her self-education, however, is astonishing. Websites featuring her story are *http://www.astr.ua.edu/4000ws/ didyouknow.1.html, http://www.hedylamarr.at/indexe.html,* and *http://www.inventions.org/culture/female/ lamarr.html.*

Review: Chapters 9–12

In the final student contribution in this book, Semir Mohammed details his family's journey from their native Ethiopia to Saudi Arabia and then to the United States. His story is a reminder that many students are learning English as a third or even fourth language. His ever-positive attitude is a tribute to the human spirit.

The passage "Why My Stepfather Was Court-Martialed" is based upon the World War II experiences of my own stepfather, Milton Markman, who came to class to share memories with my students. *The World of Words* is, in part, dedicated to his memory.

References

Adams, M. J., and A. C. Collins. (1979). A schema-theoretic view of reading. In *New directions in discourse processing,* edited by R. Freedle. Norwood, N.J.: Ablex.

Aleamoni, L. M., and L. Oboler. (1978). ACT versus SAT in predicting first semester GPA. *Educational and Psychological Measurement, 38,* 393–399.

Baumann, J.F., E.J. Kame'enui, and G.E. Ash. (2003). Research on vocabulary instruction: Voltaire Redux. In J. Flood, J.M. Jensen, D. Lapp, and J.R. Squire (eds.), *Handbook of research on the teaching of the English language arts,* (2nd ed. pp.752–785). Mahwah, N.J.: Erlbaum.

Botzum, W. A. (1951). A factorial study of reasoning and closure factors. *Psychometrica, 16,* 361–386.

Carey, J. (1987). *Eyewitness to history.* Cambridge, Mass.: Harvard University Press.

Davis, F. B. (1944). Fundamental factors of comprehension in reading. *Psychometrica, 9,* 185–197.

Davis, F. B. (1968). Research in comprehension in reading. *Reading Research Quarterly, 3,* 499–545.

Beck, I. L., and M. G. McKeown. (1991). Conditions of vocabulary learning. In R. Barr, M. L. Kamil, P. Mosenthal, and P. D. Pearson (Eds.), *Handbook of reading research* (Vol. 2, pp. 789–814). White Plains, N.Y.: Longman.

Daneman, M. (1991). Individual differences in reading skills. In R. Barr, M. L. Kamil, P. Mosenthal, and P. D. Pearson (Eds.), *Handbook of reading research* (Vol. 2, pp. 512–538). White Plains, N.Y.: Longman.

Hook, J. N. (1983). *The book of names.* New York: Franklin Watts.

Houston, L. N. (1980). Predicting academic achievement among specially admitted black female college students. *Educational and Psychological Measurement, 40,* 1189–1195.

Jenkins, J. R., M. L. Stein, and K. A. Wysocki. (1984). Learning vocabulary through reading. *American Educational Research Journal, 21,* 767–787.

Lansdown, S. (1991). Increasing vocabulary knowledge using direct instruction, cooperative grouping, and reading in junior high school. *Illinois Reading Council Journal, 19,* 15–21.

Lesgold, A. M., and C. A. Perfetti. (1978). Interactive processes in reading comprehension. *Discourse Processes, 1,* 323–326.

Malloch, D. C., and W. B. Michael. (1981). Predicting student grade point average at a community college: SAT, ACT scores, and measures of motivation. *Educational and Psychological Measurement, 41,* 1127–1135.

Mathiasen, R. E. (1984). Predicting college academic achievement: A research view. *College Student Learning, 18,* 380–386.

Nagy, W. E., R. C. Anderson, and P. A. Herman. (1987). Learning word meanings from context during normal reading. *American Educational Research Journal, 24,* 237–270.

Nist, S. L., and S. Olejnik. (1995). The role of context and dictionary definitions on varying levels of word knowledge. *Reading Research Quarterly, 30,* 172–193.

Readence, J. E., T. W. Bean, and R. S. Baldwin. (1998). *Content area literacy: An integrated approach* (6th ed.). Dubuque, Iowa: Kendall/Hunt.

Richek, M. A. (1988). Relating vocabulary learning to world knowledge. *Journal of Reading, 32,* 262–267.

Spiro, R. J. (1980). Constructive processes in prose comprehension and recall. In *Theoretical issues in reading comprehension,* edited by R. J. Spiro, B. C. Broce, and W. F. Brewer. Hillsdale, N.J.: Erlbaum.

Stahl, S. A. (1999). Vocabulary development. From *Reading research to practice,* Vol. 2 (Series editor J. Chall). Cambridge, Mass.: Brookline Books.

Stahl, S. A., and M. A. Fairbanks. (1986). The effects of vocabulary instruction: A model-based meta-analysis. *Review of Educational Research, 56,* 72–110.

Stahl, S. A., Richek, M. A., and Vandiver, R. J. (1991). Learning meaning through listening: A sixth-grade replication. In J. Zutell and S. McCormick (Eds.), *Learner factors/teacher factors: Issues in literacy research and instruction* (pp. 185–192). Chicago, Ill.: National Reading Conference.

Thorndike, R. L. (1973). Reading as reasoning. *Reading Research Quarterly, 9,* 135–147.

Weschler, D. (1981). *Weschler Adult Intelligence Scale.* New York: The Psychological Corporation.

Weitzman, R. A. (1982). The prediction of college achievement by the SAT and the high school record. *Journal of Educational Measurement, 19,* 179–191.

West, R.F., K.E. Stanovich, and H.R. Mitchell. (1993). Reading in the real world and its correlates. *Reading Research Quarterly, 28,* 35–50.

Zeno, S.M., S.H. Ivens, R.T. Millard, and R. Duvvuri. (1995). *Educator's word frequency guide* (print and electronic editions). Brewster, NY: Touchtone Applied Science Associates.

PART II: MASTERY TESTS

CHAPTER MASTERY TESTS

CHAPTER 1 TEST

A. Write the letter of its definition by each word in the left-hand column.

____1. alien	a.	foreign
____2. cosmopolitan	b.	opinionated
____3. capricious	c.	skillful
____4. disdain	d.	having a world view
____5. dogmatic	e.	scorn
	f.	unpredictable

B. Write in each blank the letter of the word that best completes the sentence. Use each choice only once.

a.	adroit	g.	exuberant	m.	intrepid
b.	affluent	h.	fraternal	n.	novice
c.	aficionado	i.	frugal	o.	renegade
d.	altruistic	j.	gauche	p.	stoic
e.	ascetic	k.	gullible	q.	venerable
f.	astute	l.	hypocritical		

6. The basketball _____ went across the country to attend games.

7. The _____ worker saved half of his paycheck each month.

8. My _____ brother grabbed food from someone else's plate.

9. The _____ child did not complain about the painful medical treatment.

10. Two brothers have a(n) _____ relationship.

11. The _____ teenagers shouted with excitement when the rock star came on stage.

12. The _____ refused to wear the school uniform.

13. The _____ explorer went down the wild river alone.

14. The _____ mayor had served the city for more than fifty years.

15. After winning the hundred million dollar lottery, Paul became _____.

16. The _____ child believed the story that chocolate bars grew on trees.

17. The _____ person seemed always to understand other people.

18. He led a(n) _____ life, praying often and living in poverty.

19. The _____ man spent each Saturday helping disabled children.

20. Professional basketball players are _____ at handling the ball.

CHAPTER 2 TEST

A. Write the letter of its definition by each word in the left-hand column.

_____1.   bureaucracy   a.   a person who runs a business
_____2.   attrition   b.   complex administration with many rules
_____3.   conservative   c.   favoring traditional beliefs
_____4.   consumer   d.   wearing away
_____5.   entrepreneur   e.   defining example
                              f.   buyer

B. Write in each blank the letter of the word that best completes the sentence. Use each choice only once.

a. accord   g. epitome   m. pacify
b. cartel   h. intervene   n. radical
c. catastrophe   i. liberal   o. reactionary
d. chaos   j. ludicrous   p. supplant
e. corroborate   k. media   q. thrive
f. diplomacy   l. ominous

6. The _____ often report about the lives of movie stars.

7. When two other people were able to _____ the report of the first man, we decided it was probably true.

8. A large increase in the number of divorces is a(n) _____ sign for society.

9. The company was entirely changed by the _____ reorganization.

10. Members of the _____ agreed to control the price of coffee.

11. It is _____ to think that people could grow wings and fly.

12. Most people prefer to reach a(n) _____ rather than to argue.

13. The underweight puppy was able to _____ in his loving home.

14. The library was in a state of _____ after the children pulled all of the books off the shelves.

15. Fatima was so skilled at _____ that she was able to criticize people without hurting their feelings.

16. Cindy's _____ parents allowed her to stay out later than her friends.

17. Many people consider Bill Gates to be the _____ of a successful businessman.

18. New, more powerful computers will soon _____ the old ones that we now use at our office.

19. War is a(n) _____ that kills people and destroys countries.

20. The teacher had to _____ and help the child who was struggling to open the heavy door.

CHAPTER 3 TEST

A. Write the letter of its definition by each word in the left-hand column.

____1.	prohibit	a.	noisy
____2.	enigma	b.	weaken
____3.	articulate	c.	to forbid
____4.	undermine	d.	skilled in using language
____5.	flaunt	e.	puzzle
		f.	show off

B. Write in each blank the letter of the word that best completes the sentence. Use each choice only once.

a. appall	g. contemplate	m. emulate
b. bland	h. contend	n. harass
c. chagrin	i. dynamic	o. skeptical
d. clarify	j. elated	p. thwart
e. condemn	k. elicit	
f. confrontation	l. emphatic	

6. Athletes from many different countries _____ in the Olympic games.

7. Much to my _____ my dog dug up all of my neighbor's flowers.

8. We were amazed at the energy of the _____ company president.

9. Every good citizen will _____ child abuse.

10. Seven people were hurt in the _____ between the government and the protesters.

11. The story of this brutal crime will _____ the public.

12. I tried to be _____ to show that I really meant what I said.

13. People should _____ carefully before they make a major life decision.

14. Mosquitoes _____ us by biting and buzzing in our ears.

15. Much of the audience fell asleep during the _____ presentation.

16. Our computer consultant was able to _____ the badly written directions so that we could understand them.

17. Doctors tried to _____ a response from the woman who had fainted.

18. The young woman was _____ when she won a full scholarship to the college of her choice.

19. Problems with our car may _____ our plans to drive across the country.

20. Since the young student wanted to be just like her teacher, she tried to _____ her clothes and the way she acted.

CHAPTER 4 TEST

A. Write the letter of its definition by each word in the left-hand column.

____1.	copious	a.	making less severe
____2.	mitigating	b.	extremely careful
____3.	chronological	c.	grow
____4.	meticulous	d.	no longer in use
____5.	obsolete	e.	plentiful
		f.	in order of time

B. Write in each blank the letter of the word that best completes the sentence. Use each choice only once.

a.	accolade	g.	euphemism	m.	pinnacle
b.	adulation	h.	indulge	n.	procrastinate
c.	augment	i.	jeopardize	o.	successive
d.	complacent	j.	mammoth	p.	withstand
e.	cryptic	k.	mandatory	q.	zealous
f.	cultivate	l.	perpetual		

6. Nobody could understand the _____ message.

7. When they have homework to do, children often _____ and decide to watch television first.

8. "Difference of opinion" is a(n) _____ that is often used for the word "fight."

9. The _____ building towered over everything else in the city.

10. Sometimes I like to _____ myself by staying in bed all day.

11. Monday, Tuesday, and Wednesday are _____ days of the week.

12. People who are overly satisfied with themselves may be called _____.

13. The monkey climbed all the way to the _____ of the huge tree.

14. It is difficult for some people to _____ a very cold, snowy winter.

15. Soldiers _____ their lives when they fight in wars.

16. Something that is _____ will last forever.

17. The _____ teacher worked several hours at home each night to prepare for her classes.

18. The famous actor was awarded the _____ of an Oscar for his great performance.

19. The school was able to _____ the number of books in the library by buying more.

20. When a person is driving a car, it is _____ to have a driver's license with him.

CHAPTER 5 TEST

A. Write the letter of its definition by each word element in the left-hand column.

____1.	re-	a.	self
____2.	anti-	b.	out of
____3.	im-	c.	again
____4.	ex-	d.	against
____5.	equi-	e.	not, in
		f.	equal

B. Write in each blank the letter of the word that best completes the sentence. Use each choice only once.

a.	antidote	g.	equivocal	m.	revelation
b.	antipathy	h.	exorbitant	n.	revert
c.	autonomous	i.	exploit	o.	subconscious
d.	eccentric	j.	ingenious	p.	subdue
e.	equilibrium	k.	invariably	q.	subordinate
f.	equitable	l.	reconcile		

6. The child lost his _____ and started to cry and scream.

7. Most adults are _____ and make their own decisions.

8. We are capable of bringing some _____ thoughts to full awareness.

9. Most people would consider $100 to be a(n) _____ price for a piece of paper.

10. The secretary is a(n) _____ of the boss.

11. The company president wanted to _____ her workers by making them work overtime without pay.

12. Even during summer, the _____ woman wore wool gloves.

13. The woman and her enemy felt much _____ toward each other.

14. The sun _____ rises in the east and sets in the west.

15. He invented a(n) _____ machine that would peel, cut, and slice every kind of vegetable.

16. The police were able to _____ the wild animal.

17. Mother divided the housework in a(n) _____ manner so that each child did the same amount.

18. People sometimes quit their bad habits, but then _____ back to them.

19. Because they wanted to save money, the couple had to _____ themselves to having a very small wedding.

20. The _____ to the poison saved the boy's life.

CHAPTER 6 TEST

A. Write the letter of its definition by each word element in the left-hand column.

    ____1.   nom   a.   beginning
    ____2.   viv   b.   all
    ____3.   anthrop   c.   human being
    ____4.   psych   d.   name
    ____5.   gen   e.   mind
                               f.   life

B. Write in each blank the letter of the word that best completes the sentence. Use each choice only once.

a. anthropological   g. genocide   m. psyche
b. boycott   h. martial   n. quixotic
c. chauvinism   i. maverick   o. viable
d. congenital   j. odyssey   p. vivacious
e. gargantuan   k. pandemonium
f. genesis   l. philanthropist

  6. The frightening dream disturbed Marsha's _____ .

  7. The student was a(n) _____ who refused to obey school rules.

  8. Maria's plan to get a job was not _____ because she could not find daycare for her children.

  9. Rachel's _____ personality helped her to get a job entertaining at children's parties.

10. _____ broke loose in the pet store when 300 birds escaped from their cages.

11. A(n) _____ gave the university money for a new building.

12. The _____ of modern theater is found in ancient Greek plays of 2,500 years ago.

13. The doctor operated to correct the baby's _____ hearing problems.

14. The _____ building is 300 stories high.

15. Because of his _____ , he felt that his country was always right.

16. The famous professor did his _____ research on the native peoples of Australia.

17. Ted took classes in _____ arts so that he could defend himself.

18. People decided to _____ the store, and they refused to buy anything there.

19. Our _____ around the world ended in Africa.

20. In a terrible act of _____ , the evil ruler killed all the people of one religion.

Name _____ Date _____

CHAPTER 7 TEST

A. Write the letter of its definition by each word element in the left-hand column.

____1.	stat	a.	turn
____2.	duc	b.	across
____3.	circum	c.	lead
____4.	trans-	d.	around
____5.	vert	e.	pull
		f.	standing

B. Write in each blank the letter of the word that best completes the sentence. Use each choice only once.

a.	abstain	g.	extract	m.	status quo
b.	circumscribe	h.	inadvertently	n.	tenable
c.	circumspect	i.	jettison	o.	tenacious
d.	circumvent	j.	perverse	p.	transcend
e.	deduction	k.	retract	q.	transitory
f.	distraught	l.	stature		

6. We added a few drops of vanilla _____ to make the cake taste better.

7. I _____ left my wallet at home when I went shopping.

8. In order to empty your stomach, you must _____ from food for twenty-four hours.

9. The man was _____ when he realized that his expensive watch was missing.

10. The rain was _____, and the sun was soon out again.

11. Because she was afraid of change, she preferred to preserve the _____.

12. The people of the country thought that the president was too powerful, so they voted to _____ his power.

13. The prisoner was able to _____ the guards and escape from jail.

14. The badly dressed, barefoot people on the street led to the _____ that this was a poor section of town.

15. The _____ executive was careful to follow all of the company rules.

16. Helen Keller was able to _____ blindness and deafness to complete an education and write books.

17. The football player's grip on the ball was so _____ that the referee had to force it out of his hand.

18. I decided to _____ some things from my backpack so that it would be lighter.

19. Albert Einstein was a scientist of great _____.

20. Just to be difficult, the _____ woman refused to take any of the medicines her doctor had recommended.

CHAPTER 8 TEST

A. Write the letter of its definition by each word element in the left-hand column.

_____1.   co-   a.   scatter
_____2.   dis-   b.   apart
_____3.   greg   c.   together
_____4.   sperse   d.   flock
                          e.   same

B. Write in each blank the letter of the word that best completes the sentence. Use each choice only once.

a. bravado   g. contemporary   m. gregarious
b. cliché   h. cuisine   n. nadir
c. coherent   i. discord   o. segregate
d. collaborate   j. disparity   p. sparse
e. communal   k. disperse   q. synopsis
f. congregate   l. disreputable   r. synthesis

5. Hundreds of runners will _____ at the starting line to begin the race.

6. My grandmother was a(n) _____ of John F. Kennedy, and she went to many of his speeches.

7. The student's paper was _____, clear, and well argued.

8. The principal felt it was not right to _____ the younger children from the older children on the playground.

9. We read a short _____ of the plot before we read the book.

10. Trees and grass are _____ in the desert.

11. The band's music is a(n) _____ of pop, reggae, and rap traditions.

12. _____ people love to spend time with others.

13. We were glad that we had decided not to do business with the _____ lawyer.

14. Many people think that Thai _____ is delicious.

15. Three fifth-grade students will _____ on one science project.

16. If you don't put the leaves in a bag after you have gathered them, the wind will _____ them.

17. Because of the _____ in the committee, members were often rude and unpleasant.

18. Anyone from the neighborhood can use the _____ tennis courts.

19. The sick, homeless woman was at the _____ of her life.

20. There is a great _____ of wealth between a millionaire and a person on welfare.

CHAPTER 9 TEST

A. Write the letter of its definition by each word element in the left-hand column.

____1. tri-
____2. ambi-
____3. ann
____4. mega-
____5. dec-

a. measure
b. both
c. three
d. large
e. year
f. ten

B. Write in each blank the letter of the word that best completes the sentence. Use each choice only once.

a. ambiguous
b. ambivalence
c. annals
d. centennial
e. centigrade
f. decimal

g. decimate
h. dilemma
i. disintegrate
j. duplicity
k. integrity
l. magnanimous

m. magnitude
n. monopoly
o. perennial
p. symmetrical
q. trilogy
r. trivial

6. In some countries, the government has a(n) _____ on all oil production.

7. Day lilies and peonies are examples of _____ flowers that bloom year after year.

8. The _____ of history record the bravery of Robert Scott, who died exploring the South Pole.

9. The temperature on top of Mount Washington dropped to 20 degrees below zero on the _____ scale.

10. Nina was _____, and decided to forgive the girls who had teased her and invite them to her party.

11. The hairstylist checked my cut to make sure it was perfectly _____ on both sides.

12. The huge blue whale is an animal of great _____.

13. After long exposure to the air, iron will _____ into a rusty powder.

14. Chen read the three books in the _____ in less than a week.

15. Rebecca was faced with the _____ of getting a divorce or staying in a marriage without love.

16. A person of _____ does not lie or cheat.

17. We were shocked by the _____ of the man who dated lonely women and then stole their money.

18. Sewing on a button is a(n) _____ task to an experienced tailor.

19. Her _____ toward school led her to enroll in college, but not attend many classes.

20. The picture was _____; it could be seen as either a vase or a face.

CHAPTER 10 TEST

A. Write the letter of its definition by each word element in the left-hand column.

_____1.   de-   a.   truth
_____2.   fid   b.   down, removal from
_____3.   cred   c.   fear
_____4.   -phobia   d.   not
_____5.   ver   e.   believe
                                 f.   faith

B. Write in each blank the letter of the word that best completes the sentence. Use each choice only once.

a.   acrophobia   g.   deviate   m.   nondescript
b.   behind the eight ball h. fidelity   n.   star-crossed
c.   claustrophobia   i.   fiduciary   o.   verify
d.   credibility   j.   hold out an olive branch p.   veritable
e.   creeds   k.   incredulity   q.   xenophobia
f.   defiant   l.   nonchalant

6. Jean had a mild case of _____ and did not like to sit in balconies.

7. Although the _____ box looked just like many other boxes, a very valuable ring was inside.

8. People with _____ sometimes find it hard to be in small, crowded rooms.

9. The school nurse called Brian's house to _____ that he was really sick.

10. Mary expressed _____ when told that people swam in the river when there was snow on the ground.

11. Colombian government leaders wanted to _____ to rebels in order to stop the fighting.

12. Many religious _____ require people to do good deeds.

13. If you _____ from the recipe, the cake you make may not taste good.

14. My grandmother was a(n) _____ treasure of old stories about the family.

15. If you tell too many lies, your _____ will be destroyed.

16. Because she had missed so many rehearsals, the actress felt she was _____.

17. Many members of my _____ family have died at very young ages.

18. The painting was copied with great _____, so the copy looked just like the original.

19. The movie star's _____ agent handled all of her financial matters.

20. The firefighter was _____ about danger, and never afraid of entering a burning building.

CHAPTER 11 TEST

A. Write the letter of its definition by each word element in the left-hand column.

____1.	spec	a.	bad, harmful
____2.	mal-	b.	without
____3.	ped	c.	hearing
____4.	bene-	d.	good
____5.	an-	e.	foot
		f.	look

B. Write in each blank the letter of the word that best completes the sentence. Use each choice only once.

a.	anarchy	g.	beneficial	m.	inaudible
b.	anonymous	h.	biodegradable	n.	malevolent
c.	apathy	i.	biopsy	o.	pathetic
d.	audit	j.	empathy	p.	pathology
e.	auspicious	k.	expedite	q.	symbiotic
f.	benefactor	l.	impede		

6. Barry was able to _____ the construction of the house, so he finished it early.

7. Since my father died when I was young, I have _____ for children who have lost their parents.

8. The _____ of BSE, or Mad Cow Disease, has not yet been completely determined.

9. We did not know the names of the _____ people who helped us.

10. The government wanted to _____ my financial records to make sure that I was paying enough taxes.

11. Some people believe that rainbows are a(n) _____ sign that will bring luck.

12. Since they are dependent on each other, many life forms live in _____ relationships.

13. The _____ ruler murdered thousands of his people.

14. The _____ revealed that the person did not have cancer.

15. The _____ attempts of the sick puppy to walk almost made us cry.

16. The _____ provided scholarships to several university students.

17. We always use _____ paper towels because we want to help the environment.

18. A loving family is _____ to children.

19. A broken computer will _____ a student's ability to finish assignments.

20. The teacher's voice was so soft that it was almost _____.

CHAPTER 12 TEST

A. Write the letter of its definition by each word element in the left-hand column.

____1.	dict	a.	voice
____2.	voc	b.	speak
____3.	script	c.	health
____4.	-logy	d.	write
		e.	study of

B. Write in each blank the letter of the word that best completes the sentence. Use each choice only once.

a. affect	g. edict	m. infer
b. colloquial	h. effect	n. invoke
c. conscious	i. epigram	o. manuscript
d. contradict	j. graphic	p. prologue
e. demographic	k. imply	q. transcribe
f. dictator	l. inscription	r. vociferous

5. When the rescue crew reached him, Carl had passed out and was no longer _____.

6. "Yeah" is a(n) _____ way to say "yes."

7. The club secretary was asked to _____ every word of the important speech.

8. The town government issued a(n) _____ that no one could smoke in a public place.

9. The description of life in India was so _____ that we felt we actually could see the towns and villages.

10. When we see dark clouds, we often _____ that it is going to rain.

11. The _____ had complete control over the country.

12. The _____ student made a loud, one-hour speech about the need for better food in the cafeteria.

13. Acid rain has a harmful _____ on forests.

14. "Might makes right" is an example of a(n) _____.

15. When two sets of directions _____ each other, people often get lost.

16. The priest will _____ the aid of God to help the people.

17. If you read the _____ to the novel, you will understand the book better.

18. A smile on your face will _____ that you are happy.

19. According to the latest _____ survey, people are getting married later than they used to.

20. The pages of the hundred-year-old _____ were yellow with age.

HALF-CHAPTER MASTERY TESTS

CHAPTER 1, PART 1 TEST

A. Write the letter of its definition by each word in the left-hand column.

____1.	fraternal	a.	unselfish
____2.	adroit	b.	unpredictable
____3.	capricious	c.	like a brother
____4.	venerable	d.	old and worthy of respect
		e.	skillful

B. Write in each blank the letter of the word that best completes the sentence. Use each choice only once.

a.	adroit	d.	ascetic	g.	gullible
b.	aficionado	e.	cosmopolitan	h.	intrepid
c.	altruistic	f.	disdain	i.	venerable

5. The opera _____ traveled around the world to see performances.

6. The _____ man approached the lion without fear.

7. The _____ woman had lived all over the world.

8. The owner of the new Lexus felt only _____ for people who drove old cars.

9. The _____ man gave thousands of dollars to charity.

10. Only a very _____ person would believe the story that cows give chocolate milk.

CHAPTER 1, PART 2 TEST

A. Write the letter of its definition by each word in the left-hand column.

_____1. astute   a. opinionated
_____2. amicable   b. enthusiastic
_____3. exuberant   c. clumsy
_____4. dogmatic   d. friendly
                           e. shrewd

B. Write in each blank the letter of the word that best completes the sentence. Use each choice only once.

a. affluent   d. exuberant   g. novice
b. alien   e. frugal   h. renegade
c. candid   f. gauche   i. stoic

5. The office worker was a(n) _____ who would not follow his boss's orders.

6. When you ask for a(n) _____ answer, you had better be prepared to hear the truth.

7. The _____ wanted to become a U.S. citizen.

8. The owner of this large and beautiful house is probably _____.

9. The _____ driver got his license only a month ago.

10. The _____ man picked up his soup bowl and started to drink from it at a formal dinner.

CHAPTER 2, PART 1 TEST

A. Write the letter of its definition by each word in the left-hand column.

_____1. attrition   a. agreement
_____2. accord   b. great disaster
_____3. media   c. means of communication
_____4. catastrophe   d. the process of wearing away gradually
                           e. administration by people who follow fixed rules

B. Write in each blank the letter of the word that best completes the sentence. Use each choice only once.

a. accord   d. catastrophe   g. entrepreneur
b. bureaucracy   e. consumer   h. intervene
c. cartel   f. corroborate   i. pacify

5. Within a few years, the immigrant became a successful _____ who owned two businesses.

6. In order to _____ the angry customer, the restaurant gave her a free meal.

7. A sugar _____ controlled prices throughout the world.

8. Cell phones that are easy to use appeal to the _____.

9. When we saw how dangerous the fight was becoming, we decided to _____ and stop it.

10. There was so much _____ at the company that ten people had to sign every letter before it could be sent.

CHAPTER 2, PART 2 TEST

A. Write the letter of its definition by each word in the left-hand column.

____1.	radical	a.	to grow
____2.	thrive	b.	favoring great change
____3.	conservative	c.	confusion
____4.	epitome	d.	favoring traditional beliefs
		e.	defining example

B. Write in each blank the letter of the word that best completes the sentence. Use each choice only once.

a. apprehend	d. liberal	g. radical
b. chaos	e. ludicrous	h. reactionary
c. defer	f. ominous	i. supplant

5. The bride's unhappiness at her wedding was a(n) _____ sign for the future of the marriage.

6. A special police force was assigned to _____ the dangerous killer.

7. The couple decided to _____ their marriage until they had enough money to buy a house.

8. With children running and shouting, the classroom was in a state of _____.

9. The _____ politician was against any type of social progress.

10. The fast food chain decided to _____ some of its most fattening food with healthier items.

CHAPTER 3, PART 1 TEST

A. Write the letter of its definition by each word in the left-hand column.

_____ 1.	dynamic	a.	noisy	
_____ 2.	confrontation	b.	energetic	
_____ 3.	concise	c.	short	
_____ 4.	boisterous	d.	hostile meeting	
		e.	very happy	

B. Write in each blank the letter of the word that best completes the sentence. Use each choice only once.

a. bland	d. elated	g. enigma
b. clarify	e. emphatic	h. skeptical
c. dynamic	f. emulate	i. thwart

5. The woman was _____ when she won an Olympic gold medal for figure skating.

6. An ice storm would _____ our plans to climb a mountain.

7. White bread and rice are _____ foods.

8. Strong opinions are often stated in a(n) _____ manner.

9. We asked our teacher to _____ the assignment because we didn't understand it.

10. The boy tried to _____ his older brother's success at school.

CHAPTER 3, PART 2 TEST

A. Write the letter of its definition by each word in the left-hand column.

____1.	flaunt	a.	to shock
____2.	belligerent	b.	to forbid
____3.	prohibit	c.	to show off
____4.	elicit	d.	hostile
		e.	to draw forth

B. Write in each blank the letter of the word that best completes the sentence. Use each choice only once.

a.	appall	d.	contemplate	g.	harass
b.	articulate	e.	contend	h.	prohibit
c.	chagrin	f.	flaunt	i.	undermine

5. Much to my _____, my child told embarrassing stories about me to the neighbors.

6. Too much alcohol can _____ your health.

7. The _____ politician was able to speak very clearly.

8. Sometimes I like to sit and _____ what my life will be like ten years from now.

9. This dangerous workplace will _____ the government inspectors.

10. Debaters from several schools will _____ in the contest.

CHAPTER 4, PART 1 TEST

A. Write the letter of its definition by each word in the left-hand column.

____1.	jeopardize	a.	mysterious in meaning
____2.	chivalrous	b.	having qualities of honor
____3.	zealous	c.	extremely enthusiastic
____4.	indulge	d.	to risk
		e.	to yield to desires

B. Write in each blank the letter of the word that best completes the sentence. Use each choice only once.

a.	accolade	d.	complacent	g.	meticulous
b.	augment	e.	indulge	h.	obsolete
c.	chivalrous	f.	mandatory	i.	cryptic

5. It is _____ that drivers stop at red lights.

6. When the student became _____ and stopped studying, his grades dropped.

7. The _____ worker carefully checked every detail.

8. The famous scientist received the _____ of the Nobel Prize.

9. I would like to _____ the amount of money in my savings account.

10. Since we no longer use feathers as pens, this custom is _____.

CHAPTER 4, PART 2 TEST

A. Write the letter of its definition by each word in the left-hand column.

_____1.   euphemism   a.   to grow
_____2.   accelerate   b.   plentiful
_____3.   copious   c.   to speed up
_____4.   successive   d.   following one after another
                                e.   a more positive word substituted for a negative word

B. Write in each blank the letter of the word that best completes the sentence. Use each choice only once.

a. accelerate   d. chronological   g. pinnacle
b. adulation   e. mammoth   h. procrastinate
c. cultivate   f. mitigating   i. withstand

5. This _____ mountain is the largest in the world.

6. People showed their _____ of the famous basketball player by standing and clapping when he came on the court.

7. In _____ order, the year 1945 comes before the year 1946.

8. I would like my car to _____ faster so that I could pass other cars more easily.

9. The farmer decided to _____ corn on his farmland.

10. Although he was guilty of doing wrong, there were _____ circumstances that helped excuse his bad behavior.

CHAPTER 5, PART 1 TEST

A. Write the letter of its definition by each word element in the left-hand column.

_____1.   equi-   a.   back, again
_____2.   sub-   b.   equal
_____3.   re-   c.   against
                            d.   under

B. Write in each blank the letter of the word that best completes the sentence. Use each choice only once.

a. equivocal   d. equitable   g. revert
b. antithesis   e. reconcile   h. subdue
c. equilibrium   f. revelation   i. subordinate

4. The city was shocked by the _____ that the trusted doctor was a drug addict.

5. The army general wanted to _____ the enemy and win the war.

6. Good is the _____ of evil.

7. After her serious car accident, Sulyema had to _____ herself to using a wheelchair.

8. We thought that the _____ decision was fair to everyone.

9. A private in the army is _____ to a captain.

10. The _____ answer could be interpreted in many different ways.

CHAPTER 5, PART 2 TEST

A. Write the letter of its definition by each word element in the left-hand column.

    _____1.   auto-   a.   out of

    _____2.   ex-   b.   against

    _____3.   in-   c.   not

                             d.   self

B. Write in each blank the letter of the word that best completes the sentence. Use each choice only once.

a.	autobiography	d.	extricate	g.	ingenious
b.	autocratic	e.	exploit	h.	interminable
c.	autonomous	f.	incongruous	i.	invariably

   4. Her cheery smile was _____ with the tragic news that she told us.

   5. It is wrong to _____ children by having them work long hours in factories or on farms.

   6. The boring, four-hour movie seemed to be _____.

   7. The office building _____ closes at 6 p.m. every day.

   8. A(n) _____ nation is not ruled by another nation.

   9. My _____ pocket PC keeps my schedule, serves as a cell phone, and takes digital photos.

 10. People worked hard to _____ the men who were caught in the mine.

CHAPTER 6, PART 1 TEST

A. Write the letter of its definition by each word element in the left-hand column.

_____1.   gen   a.   name
_____2.   viv   b.   life
_____3.   anthrop   c.   human being
                                    d.   type

B. Write in each blank the letter of the word that best completes the sentence. Use each choice only once.

a. genesis   d. philanthropist   g. viable
b. genocide   e. pseudonym   h. vital
c. misanthrope   f. renown   i. vivacious

4. The _____ hated everyone.

5. The _____ gave a million dollars for AIDS research.

6. Famous basketball champion Michael Jordan was an athlete of great _____.

7. In a terrible act of _____, the evil ruler killed all the people of one religion.

8. A supply of clean drinking water is _____ to a person's health.

9. George Eliot was the _____ used by the English writer named Marian Evans.

10. The newborn puppy was sick, but _____, and it became a healthy adult dog.

CHAPTER 6, PART 2 TEST

A. Write the letter of its definition by each word element in the left-hand column.

_____1. psych-   a. all
_____2. pan-   b. birth
                            c. mind

B. Write in each blank the letter of the word that best completes the sentence. Use each choice only once.

a. chauvinism   d. odyssey   g. psyche
b. gargantuan   e. pandemonium   h. quixotic
c. martial   f. panorama   i. spartan

3. When _____ law is declared, soldiers patrol the street to keep order.

4. The _____ flood left half of the country under water.

5. The man's hard work to establish a noble, but impossible, ideal showed that he was _____.

6. Athletes often have _____ training programs that require much self-discipline.

7. _____ broke loose when 600 students all started running at once.

8. My _____ is troubled by unhappiness.

9. The short book offered a(n) _____ of the history of art.

10. Because of his _____, the boss would not let women be executives in his company.

CHAPTER 7, PART 1 TEST

A. Write the letter of its definition by each word element in the left-hand column.

_____1.   tain   a.   placed
_____2.   duct   b.   throw
_____3.   ject   c.   hold
                        d.   lead

B. Write in each blank the letter of the word that best completes the sentence. Use each choice only once.

a.   abstain   d.   deduction   g.   stature
b.   abduction   e.   dejected   h.   tenable
c.   conducive   f.   eject   i.   tenacious

4. We thought the worker's solution for the problem was _____, and so we decided to try it.

5. Men over six feet tall are large in _____ .

6. The three year old held on to his mother's hand with a(n) _____ grip and would not let go.

7. We put fifty cents into the vending machine and watched the machine _____ a bag of potato chips.

8. After the _____ of the children, the police worked hard to get them back.

9. The man made a(n) _____ from the evidence and was able to solve the puzzle.

10. We were _____ after our vacation was suddenly cancelled.

CHAPTER 7, PART 2 TEST

A. Write the letter of its definition by each word element in the left-hand column.

____1.	trans	a.	pull
____2.	vert	b.	around
____3.	circum-	c.	across
		d.	turn

B. Write in each blank the letter of the word that best completes the sentence. Use each choice only once.

a.	adversary	d.	inadvertently	g.	transcend
b.	circumscribe	e.	perverse	h.	transformation
c.	circumvent	f.	retract	i.	transitory

4. When the man tried to _____ the line and go directly to the front counter, people in the crowd became angry.

5. The runner competed with her _____ to win the race.

6. My neighbor built a large fence to _____ his property.

7. In a(n) _____ trend, cheap used clothing became fashionable among wealthy people.

8. He was able to _____ his difficult childhood and become a happy, successful person.

9. I _____ left my keys in the car.

10. The newspaper was asked to _____ the story that was filled with errors.

CHAPTER 8, PART 1 TEST

A. Write the letter of its definition by each word element in the left-hand column.

_____1.   co-   a.   same
_____2.   dis-   b.   together
                        c.   apart

B. Write in each blank the letter of the word that best completes the sentence. Use each choice only once.

a.   collaborate   d.   contemporary   g.   disreputable
b.   communal   e.   discord   h.   syndrome
c.   concur   f.   disparity   i.   synopsis

3. After head injuries, football players can develop a post-concussion _____ that leads to problems with speech and balance.

4. We _____ with your opinion and so we will support it.

5. A _____ of the novel summarized the plot in two paragraphs.

6. In the _____ world of the 2000s, many people use cell phones.

7. The two authors will _____ to write a play.

8. There is a great _____ between the salaries of a worker and the president of a company.

9. There was much _____ in our club, so lots of time was spent arguing.

10. The back yard of the apartment building was _____ property, and so everyone was a part owner.

CHAPTER 8, PART 2 TEST

A. Write the letter of its definition by each word element in the left-hand column.

_____1. greg   a.   flock
_____2. sperse   b.   scatter

B. Write in each blank the letter of the word that best completes the sentence. Use each choice only once.

a. bravado   d. cuisine   g. segregate
b. cliché   e. intersperse   h. sparse
c. congregate   f. nadir   i. zenith

3. People often _____ at church on Sundays.

4. At the _____ of his career, the executive ran a large, successful company.

5. In an act of _____, the gang member dared his rivals to shoot at him.

6. The _____ of the man's life was when he got divorced and lost his job.

7. Farmers will _____ the sick cows from the healthy cows.

8. Italian _____ uses foods such as tomato sauce, fish, and pasta.

9. His medical treatments made him lose hair, and so the hair on his head became _____.

10. Television networks _____ programs with advertisements.

CHAPTER 9, PART 1 TEST

A. Write the letter of its definition by each word element in the left-hand column.

_____1.   du-   a.   three
_____2.   dec-   b.   one
_____3.   tri-   c.   two
                          d.   ten

B. Write in each blank the letter of the word that best completes the sentence. Use each choice only once.

a.   bilingual   d.   duplicity   g.   trivial
b.   bipartisan   e.   monarchy   h.   unanimity
c.   dilemma   f.   trilogy   i.   unilateral

4. The man was caught in the _____ of either missing work or leaving his sick mother alone.

5. Earth Day receives _____ support from both Democrats and Republicans.

6. Parents, teachers, and psychologists displayed _____ in agreeing that the troubled child needed help.

7. The _____ woman spoke Spanish and Vietnamese.

8. The mother felt that playing cards and basketball were _____ pastimes, and she wished her son would do something more important.

9. Acting alone, the principal made a(n) _____ decision to replace all the desks in all of the classrooms.

10. Saudi Arabia is a(n) _____ ruled by a king.

CHAPTER 9, PART 2 TEST

A. Write the letter of its definition by each word element in the left-hand column.

_____1. integer-
_____2. -meter
_____3. cent-

a. measure
b. large
c. whole
d. hundred

B. Write in each blank the letter of the word that best completes the sentence. Use each choice only once.

a. ambiguous
b. ambivalence
c. centennial

d. disintegrate
e. integrity
f. magnitude

g. metric
h. perennial
i. symmetrical

4. Sanjay felt some _____ toward his very strict, but loving father.

5. Pollution is a(n) _____ problem in cities that have lots of industry.

6. Since our club started in 1910, it will celebrate its _____ in 2010.

7. The statement "They are flying planes" is _____ because it has two meanings.

8. The _____ system can be used to measure distance.

9. If we are not careful, our peaceful meeting will _____ into a fight.

10. The poor student showed his _____ by returning the wallet filled with money to its owner.

CHAPTER 10, PART 1 TEST

A. Write the letter of its definition by each word element in the left-hand column.

____1.	-phobia	a.	truth
____2.	cred	b.	fear of
____3.	ver	c.	faith
		d.	belief

B. Write in each blank the letter of the word that best completes the sentence. Use each choice only once.

a.	acrophobia	d.	creeds	g.	veritable
b.	claustrophobia	e.	fidelity	h.	verify
c.	credibility	f.	fiduciary	i.	xenophobia

4. The people who managed the money of the company had _____ responsibility.

5. She was loyal and showed great _____ to her friends and family.

6. Because he suffered from _____ he was very much afraid when he was accidentally locked in the small room.

7. The doctor's _____ was destroyed when people found out he hadn't graduated from medical school.

8. The stacks of old letters were a(n) _____ history of people's lives during World War II.

9. Because of her _____, she could not look out an airplane window.

10. The registration office looked up Jonah's name in the university records to _____ that he was a student.

CHAPTER 10, PART 2 TEST

A. Write the letter of its definition by each word element in the left-hand column.

_____1.   de-   a.   faith
_____2.   non-   b.   down, removal from
                                       c.   not

B. Write in each blank the letter of the word that best completes the sentence. Use each choice only once.

a.   behind the eight ball   e.   hold out an olive branch   h.   nondescript
b.   destitute   f.   nonchalant   i.   star-crossed
c.   deviate   g.   nondenominational   j.   tongue-in-cheek
d.   leave no stone unturned

3. If you _____ from the instructions in the manual, you may not be able to install the program.

4. The man will _____ to his enemy in hopes of making peace.

5. The _____ woman often seemed to have bad luck.

6. The _____ woman had no money for food, clothing, or a place to live.

7. The spy was _____ about danger, and he never appeared to be afraid.

8. Since I missed the first two classes in the course, I felt I was _____.

9. At the _____ chapel, people from all different faiths worshiped together.

10. His appearance was so _____ that it was hard to remember what he looked like.

CHAPTER 11, PART 1 TEST

A. Write the letter of its definition by each word element in the left-hand column.

_____1.   audi   a.   foot
_____2.   spec   b.   hear
_____3.   patho   c.   look
                               d.   feeling, illness

B. Write in each blank the letter of the word that best completes the sentence. Use each choice only once.

a. audit   d. conspicuous   g. impede
b. auditory   e. empathy   h. introspection
c. auspicious   f. expedite   i. pathology

4. _____ is the process of examining our own feelings.

5. The bush with bright pink flowers was _____ in the field of green bushes.

6. We use our _____ system to hear sounds.

7. Since I have had some bad luck, I have _____ for the bad luck you have suffered.

8. The couple felt that the beautiful weather on their wedding day was a(n) _____ sign for their marriage.

9. We can _____ our car trip if we avoid traffic.

10. Heavy traffic will _____ one's progress on a trip.

CHAPTER 11, PART 2 TEST

A. Write the letter of its definition by each word element in the left-hand column.

    _____1. bio-   a. good
    _____2. bene-   b. without
    _____3. a-   c. life
                              d. harmful

B. Write in each blank the letter of the word that best completes the sentence. Use each choice only once.

    a. anarchy   d. benefactor   g. biopsy
    b. anonymous   e. beneficial   h. malevolent
    c. apathy   f. biodegradable   i. symbiotic

    4. The _____ gave several million dollars to the university.

    5. The composer of the musical piece is listed as _____ because we do not know who it is.

    6. In a(n) _____ relationship, two types of living things depend on each other.

    7. Exercise is _____ to our health.

    8. With no teacher to control the children, students were running around the room and the class was in a state of _____.

    9. The _____ revealed that the person did not have cancer.

    10. Your evil deeds show that you are _____.

CHAPTER 12, PART 1 TEST

A. Write the letter of its definition by each word element in the left-hand column.

_____1.   voc   a.   write
_____2.   dict   b.   voice
_____3.   -logy   c.   speak
                         d.   study of

B. Write in each blank the letter of the word that best completes the sentence. Use each choice only once.

a.   advocate   d.   dictator   g.   revoke
b.   colloquial   e.   invoke   h.   vociferous
c.   contradict   f.   prologue

4. The _____ suddenly changed several laws in the country.

5. Clouds are often the _____ to a storm.

6. If a pilot flies in a dangerous way, the authorities should _____ his license.

7. We often use _____ speech when we talk to friends, but formal speech when we talk to our bosses and professors.

8. The _____ of rights for farm workers talked to Congress to try to get better treatment for the workers.

9. The priest will _____ the aid of God to help the people.

10. When my mother says "yes," my father will sometimes _____ her by saying "no."

CHAPTER 12, PART 2 TEST

Write in each blank the letter of the word that best completes the sentence. Use each choice only once.

a. affect	e. effect	i. infer
b. conscience	f. epigram	j. inscription
c. conscious	g. graphic	k. manuscript
d. demographic	h. imply	l. transcribe

1. Since the moon controls tides, the moon has a(n) _____ on tides.

2. If, by your speech, you _____ that you are not happy, your friends may ask you what is wrong.

3. "Haste makes waste" is an example of a(n) _____.

4. The man was able to _____ his speech into written form and publish it as a chapter in a book.

5. If I stole something, my _____ would bother me.

6. The _____ on the stone read "This building is dedicated to students."

7. The author sent the _____ to her publisher.

8. When I speak publicly, I am always _____ of the fact that people are watching me.

9. People's moods often will _____ how well they play competitive games.

10. When children cry, we can _____ that they are not happy.

REVIEW TESTS

CHAPTERS 1 THROUGH 4 TEST

A. Write the letter of its definition by each word in the left-hand column.

____1.	thwart	a.	required
____2.	gauche	b.	replace
____3.	supplant	c.	warlike
____4.	intrepid	d.	group of producers that sets prices
____5.	jeopardize	e.	make less intense; moderate
____6.	mitigate	f.	brave
____7.	belligerent	g.	lacking in social graces
____8.	cartel	h.	ruin
		i.	to risk loss or danger

B. Write in each blank the letter of the word that best completes the sentence. Use each choice only once.

a.	accelerate	g.	chivalrous	l.	fraternal	q.	pacify
b.	accord	h.	consumer	m.	hypocritical	r.	prohibit
c.	amicable	i.	copious	n.	mandatory	s.	radical
d.	boisterous	j.	defer	o.	meticulous	t.	reactionary
e.	candid	k.	dynamic	p.	novice	u.	zealous
f.	chagrin						

9. The _____ government official talked about the need for honest government, but actually took bribes from others.

10. Laws _____ the sale of liquor to children.

11. I have a(n) _____ relationship with the people who live on my street, and I often stop to chat with them.

12. The _____ politician was against all change.

13. The _____ man always opened doors for women.

14. Please give me your _____ opinion; I want to hear the truth.

15. A(n) _____ usually looks for the best price.

16. To her _____, Mona's dad told her boyfriend all about her problems in school.

17. We hope the mother will _____ the baby so the crying will stop.

18. If people are brothers, their relationship is said to be _____.

19. The _____ tennis player was playing for the first time.

20. There is a(n) _____ amount of water in the sea.

21. I can't have lunch with you today so let's _____ it until next week.

22. The party was so _____ that the neighbors had to call the police.

23. When we _____, we go faster.

24. The two warring countries reached a(n) _____ that enabled them to live in peace.

25. When she was putting on nail polish, she took _____ care to cover every corner of each nail.

Name _____   Date _____

CHAPTERS 5 THROUGH 8 TEST

A. Write the letter of its definition by each word in the left-hand column.

____ 1.	intersperse	a.	the present state of things
____ 2.	quixotic	b.	to scatter throughout
____ 3.	syndrome	c.	having absolute power
____ 4.	equivocal	d.	noble but not practical
____ 5.	circumspect	e.	a group of symptoms indicating a disorder
____ 6.	misanthrope	f.	showing bravery
____ 7.	autocratic	g.	careful
____ 8.	status quo	h.	doubtful
		i.	a person who hates or distrusts others

B. Write in each blank the letter of the word that best completes the sentence. Use choices only once.

a.	adversary	g.	compatible	m.	psychosomatic
b.	antithesis	h.	concur	n.	revelation
c.	autobiography	i.	conducive	o.	spartan
d.	charisma	j.	dejected	p.	transformation
e.	circumscribe	k.	extricate	q.	vital
f.	cliché	l.	nominal		

9. Mary was the _____ chairperson, but Jane held all the power in the club.

10. It is _____ that human beings have air to breathe.

11. An example of a(n) _____ is "Have a nice day."

12. Right is the _____ of wrong.

13. He lived in a(n) _____ manner, without hot water or electricity.

14. A good education is _____ to getting a well-paying job.

15. It is almost impossible to _____ the last bit of ketchup from the jar.

16. The athlete was _____ after he lost the race.

17. A wall was built to _____ the city and protect it from attack.

18. In his _____, Benjamin Franklin gave the history of his own life.

19. We were shocked by the _____ that the mayor had stolen money from the city.

20. I fought with my _____.

21. Since the doctor could not find anything wrong physically, she thought that the illness was _____.

22. Since Margaret and Iris are _____, they spend a lot of time together.

23. The _____ in her appearance was so complete that I didn't recognize her.

24. We are delighted that you _____ with our decision and will support it.

25. The _____ of stars like Julia Roberts draws fans to the movies.

CHAPTERS 9 THROUGH 12 TEST

A. Write the letter of its definition by each word in the left-hand column.

____1.	tongue-in-cheek	a.	to say the opposite of something
____2.	colloquial	b.	fear of closed or small spaces
____3.	claustrophobia	c.	refering to informal conversation
____4.	contradict	d.	jokingly
____5.	biodegradable	e.	exclusive possession or control
____6.	bipartisan	f.	lack of interest or emotion
____7.	apathy	g.	not clear
____8.	veritable	h.	supported by members of two parties
		i.	capable of being broken down by natural processes
		j.	being truly so

B. Write in each blank the letter of the word that best completes the sentence. Use each choice only once.

a.	benefactor	g.	delude	m.	malady
b.	carte blanche	h.	expedite	n.	monologue
c.	conscience	i.	fiduciary	o.	nondenominational
d.	creed	j.	inscription	p.	star-crossed
e.	decade	k.	loquacious	q.	symmetrical
f.	defiant	l.	magnanimous	r.	veracity

9. As soon as the small boy stole the watch, his _____ began to bother him.

10. The _____ man forgave those who had insulted him.

11. The _____ baseball player refused to follow the orders of his coach.

12. In the one-man show, the actor delivered a(n) _____.

13. The teenager was _____ and loved to talk with her friends for hours.

14. The religious woman was careful to follow the _____ of the Jewish faith.

15. Since the design is the same on both sides, it is _____.

16. Don't _____ yourself into thinking that you can run a long race without training and practice.

17. I would like to have _____ to spend as much money as I wanted.

18. The _____ kept me in bed for a few days.

19. Since we think you may be telling a lie, we doubt the _____ of your statement.

20. The _____ place to pray welcomed people of all religions.

21. During the _____ between 1930 and 1940, the U.S. economy was in a depression.

22. The money to pay for the museum was given by a(n) _____.

23. The _____ was given authority over financial matters.

24. The _____ inside the book read, "To my son, with love."

25. If we walk faster, we can _____ our progress.

CHAPTERS 1 THROUGH 6 TEST

A. Write the letter of its definition by each word in the left-hand column.

_____ 1. supplant	a.	to weaken
_____ 2. undermine	b.	of lesser importance
_____ 3. perpetual	c.	truthful
_____ 4. subordinate	d.	prevent from happening
_____ 5. candid	e.	very large
_____ 6. defer	f.	to replace
_____ 7. liberal	g.	lasting forever
_____ 8. intrepid	h.	brave
_____ 9. subconscious	i.	lively
_____10. gargantuan	j.	to delay
	k.	favoring gradual progress and reform
	l.	beneath awareness

B. Write in each blank the letter of the word that best completes the sentence. Use each choice only once.

a.	abduction	e.	cliché	i.	epitome
b.	apprehend	f.	congenital	j.	incongrous
c.	autonomous	g.	contemplate	k.	indulge
d.	chivalrous	h.	enigma	l.	psychosomatic

11. The _____ knight carefully followed his code of honor and maintained respect for women.

12. The old, worn-out furniture seemed _____ with the beautiful, modern apartment.

13. No one knows the answer to this _____.

14. The man had been born with a(n) _____ heart problem.

15. That wonderful athlete is the _____ of a great soccer player.

16. A person may decide to _____ herself by taking a wonderful vacation.

17. I must _____ the matter carefully before I make a decision.

18. The police were able to _____ the man who had escaped from jail.

19. We have all heard the _____ "waste not, want not" many times.

20. The law considers _____ to be a serious crime.

Learning Strategies

C. *Knowledge*   Write the letter of the choice that best completes each sentence.

_____21. The prefix *pan-* means
           a. not.   b. human.   c. life.   d. all.

_____22. The prefix *ex-* means
           a. equal.   b. again.   c. out of.   d. in.

_____23. The prefix *anti-* means
           a. against.   b. together.   c. self.   d. under.

_____24. The root *gen* means
           a. birth.   b. life.   c. human being.   d. equal.

_____25. An etymology listed as [ME<OE<L] shows that the word was first recorded in
    a. Latin.   b. French.   c. Greek.   d. Old English.

_____26. If a verb entry in a dictionary has an adverb form,
    a. the adverb form always has a separate entry.
    b. the adverb form never appears in the dictionary.
    c. the adverb form is usually listed under the verb.

D. *Application*   Write the letter of the choice that best defines the italicized word in each sentence.

_____27. On the hike, the man held his water in a *haversack*.
    a. car   b. bag   c. sink   d. lake

_____28. A sea is an *aqueous* place.
    a. filled with water   b. filled with trees   c. filled with air   d. filled with animals

_____29. The *thespian* performed in the theater.
    a. writer   b. actor   c. child   d. curtain

_____30. The growth was *exogenous* to the animal.
    a. starting suddenly   b. starting inside   c. starting outside   d. starting slowly

_____31. Her *raucous* laughter was a contrast to her pleasant, quiet speech.
    a. soft   b. beautiful   c. nice   d. harsh

_____32. We didn't believe a word of his *cant*.
    a. funny statements.   b. difficult statements   c. true statements   d. silly talk

_____33. Something that is *substandard* is
    a. against standard.   b. normal about standard.   c. below standard.
    d. the opposite of standard.

CHAPTERS 7 THROUGH 12 TEST

A. Write the letter of its definition by each word in the left-hand column.

_____ 1. dejected   a. not associated with one religion
_____ 2. extract   b. to draw or pull out
_____ 3. xenophobia   c. accidentally
_____ 4. advocate   d. noticeable
_____ 5. circumvent   e. to throw out
_____ 6. trivial   f. good moral character
_____ 7. contemporary   g. to avoid
_____ 8. nondenominational   h. depressed
_____ 9. conspicuous   i. not important
_____ 10. integrity   j. existing at the same time
                              k. to urge publicly
                              l. fear of foreigners

B. Write in each blank the letter of the word that best completes the sentence. Use each choice only once.

a. centennial   g. imply
b. decimate   h. inaudible
c. destitute   i. infer
d. discord   j. monarchy
e. ecology   k. trivial
f. give carte blanche l. transformation

11. He made a complete _____ from an evil person into a good one.

12. Because there was so much _____ among my family members, our meals often ended in fights.

13. If you _____ that I have told a lie, I will become angry.

14. The _____ of the area was disturbed when all the trees were cut down.

15. The country of Great Britain is a(n) _____ that is ruled by a queen.

16. The club was started in 1905 and it celebrated its _____ in 2005.

17. When he lost all of his money, the man was left _____.

18. We could not hear the _____ sound.

19. Adding two and two would be a(n) _____ task for a mathematician.

20. I would like someone to _____ to me to spend all the money I want.

Learning Strategies

C. *Knowledge*   Write the letter of its definition by each word element in the left-hand column.

_____21.	ann	a.	one
_____22.	vert	b.	foot
_____23.	cent-	c.	turn
_____24.	ped	d.	believe
_____25.	ject	e.	ten
_____26.	cred	f.	year
_____27.	scribe	g.	write
_____28.	sperse	h.	throw
		i.	scatter
		j.	hundred

D. *Application*   Write the letter of the choice that best defines the italicized word in each sentence.

_____29. The engineers *transduced* the energy.
a. changed the energy's form   b. wanted the energy's power   c. multiplied the energy's power
d. decreased the energy

_____30. People were afraid that the new spray would *defoliate* the trees.
a. cause leaves to stick together   b. cause trees to lose leaves   c. cause trees to grow larger
d. make dogs sick

_____31. She drew a *decagon* on the board.
a. figure with one side   b. figure with three sides   c. figure with ten sides
d. figure with one hundred sides

_____32. The medicine *antivert* can be taken
a. to help a person to stand up.   b. to fight against turning or dizziness.
c. to restore the ability to see.   d. to cure all illnesses.

_____33. According to legend, there are creatures called *monopodes*.
a. creatures with three lives   b. creatures with four ears   c. creatures with two eyes
d. creatures with one foot

ENTIRE BOOK TEST

A. Write the letter of its definition by each word in the left-hand column.

_____ 1. fidelity	a.	worthy of respect because of age
_____ 2. venerable	b.	short, witty saying
_____ 3. euphemism	c.	unquestionable; being truly so
_____ 4. apathy	d.	enemy, rival
_____ 5. extricate	e.	substitution of a positive word
_____ 6. loquacious	f.	lack of emotion or interest
_____ 7. panorama	g.	talkative
_____ 8. stoic	h.	view over a wide area
_____ 9. incongruous	i.	to free from difficulty
_____10. decimate	j.	to annoy or attack repeatedly
_____11. veritable	k.	out of place; not in harmony
_____12. adversary	l.	faithfulness
_____13. harass	m.	having two meanings
	n.	to destroy a large part of
	o.	not affected by pain or pleasure

B. Write in each blank the letter of the word that best completes the sentence. Use each choice only once.

a. advocate	e. bilingual	i. retract
b. anarchy	f. concise	j. status quo
c. antithesis	g. conspicuous	k. synthesis
d. attrition	h. radical	l. withstand

14. Since I am a(n) _____ of public education, I would like to spend more money on schools.

15. The _____ teacher used both English and Spanish when she taught her students.

16. Hate is the _____ of love.

17. The tall building was _____ in the neighborhood filled with small homes.

18. We expect the country's leader to _____ her false statement.

19. The perfume was a(n) _____ of flowers, spices, and oil.

20. After he made his paper more _____ it took less time to type.

21. Through a process of _____ due to rain and snow, the bricks on the house wore away.

22. The country had no law or order; it was in a state of _____.

23. People find is difficult to _____ the stress in their lives.

Name _____ Date _____

C. Write in each blank the letter of the word that best completes the sentence. Use each choice only once.

a. affluent   e. introspection   i. nominal
b. alien   f. magnitude   j. obsolete
c. auditory   g. malpractice   k. syndrome
d. decimate   h. meticulous   l. transitory

24. Important scientists such as Copernicus and Galileo made discoveries of great _____.

25. A disease called Tourette's _____ causes symptoms including loud speech, anger, and uncontrolled movements.

26. The _____ couple owned two homes and two new cars.

27. The _____ student checked his paper carefully to make sure that each answer was correct.

28. During moments of _____, we think about our own lives.

29. The doctor who ruined her patient's health was accused of _____.

30. The spinning wheel is now _____ because more modern tools have been invented for making thread.

31. The man was a(n) _____, but he wanted to become a citizen.

32. A terrible disease can _____ the population of a country.

33. The king is the _____ head of the government, but the prime minister holds most of the power.

Learning Strategies

D. *Dictionary use*   Write the letter of the choice that best completes each sentence.

_____34. When the word *Chem.* appears in italics before one definition in a dictionary entry, it shows that
a. there is no special usage of the word.
b. all the definitions are used only in the field of chemistry.
c. one definition of the word is used in the field of chemistry.
d. the word is never used in the field of chemistry.

_____35. After you use context clues to figure out the meaning of a word, you can use a dictionary if you
a. need to keep reading.   b. want to save time.   c. want to determine an exact meaning.
d. don't want to find the meaning.

_____36. The etymology of a word refers to its
a. meaning.   b. part of speech.   c. origin.   d. pronunciation.

E. *Context clues*   Using context clues, write the letter of the definition of the italicized word in each sentence.

_____37. People feared the effects of the *noxious* chemical.
a. smelly   b. excellent   c. rare   d. harmful

_____38. Others may have thought that this vocabulary course was not needed, but we thought it was *requisite* for success in college.
a. bad   b. necessary   c. hopeful   d. unnecessary

_____39. We saw the *marino* eating grass on the hill.
a. sheep   b. fish   c. house   d. man

_____40. We stepped in a *gingerly* fashion so that we would not lose our balance.
a. cautious   b. dance   c. fast   d. hopping

_____ 41. Her quiet manner was a contrast to her brother's *bumptious* one.
　　　a. silent　　　b. noisy　　　c. successful　　　d. hopeful

F.　*Word elements*　Using your knowledge of word elements, write the letter of the answer that defines the italicized word or best replaces each blank.

_____ 42. They were specialists in *biometrics*.
　　　a. measuring living things　　　b. feelings of people　　　c. measuring vision　　　d. feeling or belief

_____ 43. The meaning of the word element *ped-* is ___.
　　　a. good　　　b. without　　　c. foot　　　d. hear

_____ 44. The meaning of the word element *anthrop-* is ___.
　　　a. not　　　b. feeling　　　c. human　　　d. together

_____ 45. My film was *panchromatic*.
　　　a. having one color　　　b. having no colors　　　c. having equal colors　　　d. having all colors

_____ 46. The meaning of the word element *ver* is ___.
　　　a. truth　　　b. fear　　　c. not　　　d. belief

_____ 47. The doctor made an *audiogram* during the examination.
　　　a. written record of hearing　　　b. spoken record of vision　　　c. good record of speech
　　　d. fast record of walking

_____ 48. The meaning of the word element *dec-* is ___.
　　　a. ten　　　b. hundred　　　c. one　　　d. three

_____ 49. The meaning of the word element *tain* is ___.
　　　a. pull　　　b. hold　　　c. across　　　d. three

_____ 50. We all hoped for a *regenesis* of the talent he had shown before.
　　　a. turning back　　　b. carrying on　　　c. end to　　　d. beginning again

ANSWER KEY TO MASTERY TESTS

MASTERY TESTS

Chapter 1	1. a	2. d	3. f	4. e	5. b	6. c	7. i	8. j	9. p	10. h	11. g	12. o	13. m	14. q
	15. b	16. k	17. f	18. e	19. d	20. a								
Chapter 2	1. b	2. d	3. c	4. f	5. a	6. k	7. e	8. l	9. n	10. b	11. j	12. a	13. q	14. d
	15. f	16. i	17. g	18. p	19. c	20. h								
Chapter 3	1. c	2. e	3. d	4. b	5. f	6. h	7. c	8. i	9. e	10. f	11. a	12. l	13. g	14. n
	15. b	16. d	17. k	18. j	19. p	20. m								
Chapter 4	1. e	2. a	3. f	4. b	5. d	6. e	7. n	8. g	9. j	10. h	11. o	12. d	13. m	14. p
	15. i	16. l	17. q	18. a	19. c	20. k								
Chapter 5	1. c	2. d	3. e	4. b	5. f	6. e	7. c	8. o	9. h	10. q	11. i	12. d	13. b	14. k
	15. j	16. p	17. f	18. n	19. l	20. a								
Chapter 6	1. d	2. f	3. c	4. e	5. a	6. m	7. i	8. o	9. p	10. k	11. l	12. f	13. d	14. e
	15. c	16. a	17. h	18. b	19. j	20. g								
Chapter 7	1. f	2. c	3. d	4. b	5. a	6. g	7. h	8. a	9. f	10. q	11. m	12. b	13. d	14. e
	15. c	16. p	17. o	18. i	19. l	20. j								
Chapter 8	1. c	2. b	3. d	4. a	5. f	6. g	7. c	8. o	9. q	10. p	11. r	12. m	13. l	14. h
	15. d	16. k	17. i	18. e	19. n	20. j								
Chapter 9	1. c	2. b	3. e	4. d	5. f	6. n	7. o	8. c	9. e	10. l	11. p	12. m	13. i	14. q
	15. h	16. k	17. j	18. r	19. b	20. a								
Chapter 10	1. b	2. f	3. e	4. c	5. a	6. a	7. m	8. c	9. o	10. k	11. j	12. e	13. g	14. p
	15. d	16. b	17. n	18. h	19. i	20. l								
Chapter 11	1. f	2. a	3. e	4. d	5. b	6. k	7. j	8. p	9. b	10. d	11. e	12. q	13. n	14. i
	15. o	16. f	17. h	18. g	19. l	20. m								
Chapter 12	1. b	2. a	3. d	4. e	5. c	6. b	7. q	8. g	9. j	10. m	11. f	12. r	13. h	14. i
	15. d	16. n	17. p	18. k	19. e	20. o								

HALF-CHAPTER MASTERY TESTS

Chapter 1 Part 1	1. c	2. e	3. b	4. d	5. b	6. h	7. e	8. f	9. c	10. g
Chapter 1 Part 2	1. e	2. d	3. b	4. a	5. h	6. c	7. b	8. a	9. g	10. f
Chapter 2 Part 1	1. d	2. a	3. c	4. b	5. g	6. i	7. c	8. e	9. h	10. b
Chapter 2 Part 2	1. b	2. a	3. d	4. e	5. f	6. a	7. c	8. b	9. h	10. i
Chapter 3 Part 1	1. b	2. d	3. c	4. a	5. d	6. i	7. a	8. e	9. b	10. f
Chapter 3 Part 2	1. c	2. d	3. b	4. e	5. c	6. i	7. b	8. d	9. a	10. e
Chapter 4 Part 1	1. d	2. b	3. c	4. e	5. f	6. d	7. g	8. a	9. b	10. h
Chapter 4 Part 2	1. e	2. c	3. b	4. d	5. e	6. b	7. d	8. a	9. c	10. f
Chapter 5 Part 1	1. b	2. d	3. a	4. f	5. h	6. b	7. e	8. d	9. i	10. a
Chapter 5 Part 2	1. d	2. a	3. c	4. f	5. e	6. h	7. i	8. b	9. g	10. d
Chapter 6 Part 1	1. d	2. b	3. c	4. c	5. d	6. f	7. b	8. h	9. e	10. g
Chapter 6 Part 2	1. c	2. a	3. c	4. b	5. h	6. i	7. e	8. g	9. f	10. a
Chapter 7 Part 1	1. c	2. d	3. b	4. h	5. g	6. i	7. f	8. b	9. d	10. e

Chapter 7 Part 2	1. c	2. d	3. b	4. c	5. a	6. b	7. e	8. g	9. d	10. f
Chapter 8 Part 1	1. b	2. c	3. h	4. c	5. i	6. d	7. a	8. f	9. e	10. b
Chapter 8 Part 2	1. a	2. b	3. c	4. i	5. a	6. f	7. g	8. d	9. h	10. e
Chapter 9 Part 1	1. c	2. d	3. a	4. c	5. b	6. h	7. a	8. g	9. i	10. e
Chapter 9 Part 2	1. c	2. a	3. d	4. b	5. h	6. c	7. a	8. g	9. d	10. e
Chapter 10 Part 1	1. b	2. d	3. a	4. f	5. e	6. b	7. c	8. g	9. a	10. h
Chapter 10 Part 2	1. b	2. c	3. c	4. e	5. i	6. b	7. f	8. a	9. g	10. h
Chapter 11 Part 1	1. b	2. c	3. d	4. h	5. d	6. b	7. e	8. c	9. f	10. g
Chapter 11 Part 2	1. c	2. a	3. b	4. d	5. b	6. i	7. e	8. a	9. g	10. h
Chapter 12 Part 1	1. b	2. c	3. d	4. d	5. f	6. g	7. b	8. a	9. e	10. c
Chapter 12 Part 2	1. e	2. h	3. f	4. 1	5. b	6. j	7. k	8. c	9. a	10. i

Review Tests

Chapters 1–4 1. h 2. g 3. b 4. f 5. i 6. e 7. c 8. d 9. m 10. r 11. c 12. t 13. g
14. e 15. h 16. f 17. q 18. 1 19. p 20. i 21. j 22. d 23. a 24. b 25. o

Chapters 5–8 1. b 2. d 3. e 4. h 5. g 6. i 7. c 8. a 9. 1 10. q 11. f 12. b 13. o
14. i 15. k 16. j 17. e 18. c 19. n 20. a 21. m 22. g 23. p 24. h 25. d

Chapters 9–12 1. d 2. c 3. b 4. a 5. i 6. h 7. f 8. j 9. c 10. 1 11. f 12. n 13. k
14. d 15. q 16. g 17. b 18. m 19. r 20. o 21. e 22. a 23. i 24. j 25. h

Chapters 1–6 1. f 2. a 3. g 4. b 5. c 6. j 7. k 8. h 9. 1 10. e 11. d 12. j 13. h 14. f
15. i 16. k 17. g 18. b 19. e 20. a 21. d 22. c 23. a 24. a 25. a 26. c
27. b 28. a 29. b 30. c 31. d 32. d 33. c

Chapters 7–12 1. h 2. b 3. 1 4. k 5. g 6. i 7. j 8. a 9. d 10. f 11. 1 12. d 13. g 14. e
15. j 16. a 17. c 18. h 19. k 20. f 21. f 22. c 23. j 24. b 25. h 26. d
27. g 28. i 29. a 30. b 31. c 32. b 33. d

Entire Book

1. 1 2. a 3. e 4. f 5. i 6. g 7. h 8. o 9. k 10. n 11. c 12. d 13. j 14. a 15. e
16. c 17. g 18. i 19. k 20. f 21. d 22. b 23. 1 24. f 25. k 26. a 27. h 28. e 29. g
30. j 31. b 32. d 33. i 34. c 35. c 36. c 37. d 38. b 39. a 40. a 41. b 42. a 43. c
44. c 45. d 46. a 47. a 48. a 49. b 50. d

PART III:
SUPPLEMENTARY AND REVIEW
EXERCISES

MULTIPLE-CHOICE SENTENCES

CHAPTER 1, PART 1 SUPPLEMENTARY EXERCISE

Write in the letter of the word that best completes each sentence.

_____ 1. The _____ lived in poverty and dedicated his life to good deeds.

        a. cosmopolitan   b. aficionado   c. ascetic

_____ 2. The _____ man fought bravely against great odds.

        a. altruistic   b. intrepid   c. gullible

_____ 3. The words of the_____ man did not match his actions.

        a. hypocritical   b. fraternal   c. adroit

_____ 4. Brothers have a(n) _____ relationship.

        a. gullible   b. fraternal   c. ascetic

_____ 5. The basketball player was _____ at handling the ball.

        a. adroit   b. disdain   c. venerable

_____ 6. The snob treated other people with _____.

        a. hypocritical   b. ascetic   c. disdain

_____ 7. _____ people often change their minds.

        a. Intrepid   b. Gullible   c. Capricious

_____ 8. The _____ ruler had guided his people for sixty years.

        a. gullible   b. aficionado   c. venerable

CHAPTER 1, PART 2 SUPPLEMENTARY EXERCISE

Write in the letter of the word that best completes each sentence.

_____ 1. The _____ soldier did not complain about his pain.

        a. stoic   b. renegade   c. alien

_____ 2. The_____ man refused to change his opinion.

        a. gauche   b. amicable   c. dogmatic

_____ 3. We could not understand the _____ culture.

        a. astute   b. alien   c. amicable

_____ 4. The _____ son helped to pay his father's bills.

        a. renegade   b. affluent   c. exuberant

_____ 5. The_____ swimmer was helped by someone more experienced.

        a. dogmatic   b. candid   c. novice

_____ 6. The _____ man knew how to get his way.

        a. alien   b. frugal   c. astute

_____ 7. The _____ led a rebellion.

        a. renegade   b. exuberant   c. candid

_____ 8. The _____ person had terrible table manners.

        a. astute   b. gauche   c. dogmatic

CHAPTER 2, PART 1 SUPPLEMENTARY EXERCISE

Write in the letter of the word that best completes each sentence.

_____ 1. Telephone companies tried to form a _____ to control prices throughout the world.

   a. diplomacy   b. media   c. cartel

_____ 2. The flood was a(n) _____ that destroyed many crops.

   a. intervene   b. catastrophe   c. pacify

_____ 3. The _____ shopped carefully.

   a. media   b. bureaucracy   c. consumer

_____ 4. His _____ won him many friends.

   a. diplomacy   b. intervene   c. attrition

_____ 5. If two athletes fight, the referee will _____ and stop the quarrel.

   a. catastrophe   b. intervene   c. consumer

_____ 6. The second man was able to _____ the report of the first man.

   a. bureaucracy   b. corroborate   c. pacify

_____ 7. The _____ started a new business.

   a. entrepreneur   b. diplomacy   c. attrition

_____ 8. A skilled teacher can _____ a child who loses her temper.

   a. consumer   b. pacify   c. accord

CHAPTER 2, PART 2 SUPPLEMENTARY EXERCISE

Write in the letter of the word that best completes each sentence.

_____ 1. The teacher's frown was a(n) _____ sign for the class.

        a. epitome   b. ominous   c. liberal

_____ 2. Babe Ruth was the _____ of a great baseball player.

        a. radical   b. defer   c. epitome

_____ 3. A four-year-old would look _____ in high-heeled shoes.

        a. conservative   b. ludicrous   c. chaos

_____ 4. The _____ senator favored the rights of women and minorities.

        a. liberal   b. thrive   c. reactionary

_____ 5. I try to _____ to the judgment of people who know more than I do.

        a. thrive   b. apprehend   c. defer

_____ 6. The _____ restructuring changed everything in the company.

        a. liberal   b. radical   c. conservative

_____ 7. Horses _____ if their owners take good care of them.

        a. defer   b. apprehend   c. thrive

_____ 8. The papers were thrown all over the room in a state of _____.

        a. chaos   b. conservative   c. epitome

CHAPTER 3, PART 1 SUPPLEMENTARY EXERCISE

Write in the letter of the word that best completes each sentence.

_____ 1. My friend stated his opinions in a(n) _____ manner because he believed in them strongly.

    a. bland   b. emphatic   c. enigma

_____ 2. The police were able to _____ the planned robbery.

    a. concise   b. confrontation   c. thwart

_____ 3. The origin of the universe is a(n) _____.

    a. skeptical   b. clarify   c. enigma

_____ 4. The young boy wanted to _____ the great athlete.

    a. elated   b. dynamic   c. emulate

_____ 5. The _____ man had much energy.

    a. dynamic   b. elated   c. skeptical

_____ 6. The _____ graduation speech lasted only three minutes.

    a. concise   b. confrontation   c. elated

_____ 7. I am _____ of your ability to do that difficult task.

    a. bland   b. skeptical   c. confrontation

_____ 8. The _____ students made a lot of noise.

    a. boisterous   b. bland   c. emulate

Name _____   Date _____

CHAPTER 3, PART 2 SUPPLEMENTARY EXERCISE

Write in the letter of the word that best completes each sentence.

_____ 1. If you _____ your intelligence, other people may resent you.

    a. flaunt   b. chagrin   c. harass

_____ 2. Lack of sleep can _____ your health.

    a. articulate   b. elicit   c. undermine

_____ 3. I felt _____ when I realized the silly mistake I had made.

    a. belligerent   b. chagrin   c. condemn

_____ 4. The story of his evil crimes will _____ any decent human being.

    a. harass   b. appall   c. undermine

_____ 5. It is wise to _____ important decisions.

    a. contemplate   b. flaunt   c. condemn

_____ 6. It is sometimes difficult to _____ how you are feeling.

    a. articulate   b. belligerent   c. harass

_____ 7. We tried to _____ some talk from the parakeet.

    a. flaunt   b. harass   c. elicit

_____ 8. The two athletes will _____ in the race.

    a. elicit   b. contend   c. undermine

CHAPTER 4, PART 1 SUPPLEMENTARY EXERCISE

Write in the letter of the word that best completes each sentence.

_____ 1. Try not to _____ your health by working too hard and getting little sleep.

    a. meticulous   b. jeopardize   c. augment

_____ 2. A new rule made English 101 a(n) _____ course for everyone.

    a. indulge   b. complacent   c. mandatory

_____ 3. The _____ worshipers prayed all day.

    a. augment   b. mandatory   c. zealous

_____ 4. We could not understand the _____ directions.

    a. perpetual   b. cryptic   c. accolade

_____ 5. We should _____ our supply of emergency flares for the car.

    a. perpetual   b. mandatory   c. augment

_____ 6. _____ care is needed to keep a house clean.

    a. Obsolete   b. Meticulous   c. Chivalrous

_____ 7. The _____ man was very sure of himself.

    a. accolade   b. zealous   c. complacent

_____ 8. The _____ man always took special care to be polite to women.

    a. perpetual   b. chivalrous   c. obsolete

CHAPTER 4, PART 2 SUPPLEMENTARY EXERCISE

Write in the letter of the word that best completes each sentence.

_____ 1. His kind comment had a _____ effect on my negative view of him.

  a. mitigating   b. copious   c. withstand

_____ 2. "Superintendent" is a(n) _____ for "janitor."

  a. adulation   b. accelerate   c. euphemism

_____ 3. The _____ attacks of wind, rain, and humid air have ruined my hairdo.

  a. cultivate   b. successive   c. withstand

_____ 4. There was a(n) _____ amount of fruit juice at the picnic, so I drank several glasses.

  a. copious   b. accelerate   c. cultivate

_____ 5. The teacher covered the events of the revolution in _____ order.

  a. withstand   b. pinnacle   c. chronological

_____ 6. Students had feelings of _____ toward their wonderful professor.

  a. copious   b. adulation   c. euphemism

_____ 7. The soldiers struggled to _____ the enemy's attack.

  a. cultivate   b. mitigating   c. withstand

_____ 8. A person often tries to _____ friends who share his interests.

  a. cultivate   b. mammoth   c. accelerate

CHAPTER 5, PART 1 SUPPLEMENTARY EXERCISE

Write in the letter of the word that best completes each sentence.

_____ 1. A person who walks a tightrope must keep his _____.

   a. reconcile   b. subdue   c. equilibrium

_____ 2. Power is the _____ of weakness.

   a. subordinate   b. antithesis   c. antipathy

_____ 3. We found the _____ statement difficult to understand.

   a. revert   b. equitable   c. equivocal

_____ 4. Soldiers try to _____ their desire to run from danger.

   a. equivocal   b. subdue   c. revelation

_____ 5. I try to _____ myself to things I cannot change.

   a. reconcile   b. subconscious   c. antidote

_____ 6. Readers were shocked by the _____ in the newspaper.

   a. revelation   b. equivocal   c. equilibrium

_____ 7. The man had a(n) _____ position at the company.

   a. antithesis   b. antipathy   c. subordinate

_____ 8. The price of the stock may _____ to its original level.

   a. equitable   b. revert   c. subconscious

CHAPTER 5, PART 2 SUPPLEMENTARY EXERCISE

Write in the letter of the word that best completes each sentence.

_____ 1. In her _____, the movie star told her life story.

       a. autobiography   b. impartial   c. ingenious

_____ 2. The man was _____ and didn't favor either side in the fight.

       a. extricate   b. exorbitant   c. impartial

_____ 3. People who dress in _____ ways often receive stares from others.

       a. autocratic   b. eccentric   c. invariably

_____ 4. A person with an intelligent mind should _____ its powers by becoming educated.

       a. interminable   b. autonomous   c. exploit

_____ 5. Good social relationships are _____ with fights between friends.

       a. autocratic   b. incongruous   c. extricate

_____ 6. The scientist created an _____ machine for squeezing oranges.

       a. ingenious   b. impartial   c. invariably

_____ 7. Five dollars would be an _____ price for a safety pin.

       a. exploit   b. exorbitant   c. impartial

_____ 8. An _____ ruler would not listen to the opinions of others.

       a. incongruous   b. autocratic   c. impartial

CHAPTER 6, PART 1 SUPPLEMENTARY EXERCISE

Write in the letter of the word that best completes each sentence.

_____ 1. The important document was_____ to the project.

       a. renowned   b. vital   c. congenital

_____ 2. _____ is a terrible crime.

       a. Genesis   b. Genocide   c. Misanthrope

_____ 3. We thought the plan was _____.

       a. viable   b. philanthropist   c. vivacious

_____ 4. A(n) _____ study might deal with a tribe of people.

       a. philanthropist   b. pseudonym   c. anthropological

_____ 5. He was born with a _____ physical problem.

       a. viable   b. congenital   c. misanthrope

_____ 6. The artist used the _____ "Henry Smith."

       a. congenital   b. pseudonym   c. misanthrope

_____ 7. The _____ girl was often the center of attention.

       a. vivacious   b. genesis   c. viable

_____ 8. Because of his great deeds, the _____ of Albert Schweitzer spread throughout the world.

       a. nominal   b. renown   c. philanthropist

CHAPTER 6, PART 2 SUPPLEMENTARY EXERCISE

Write in the letter of the word that best completes each sentence.

_____ 1. His _____ routine included no luxuries.

      a. boycott   b. spartan   c. gargantuan

_____ 2. She felt _____ toward her country, certain that it was the best in the world.

      a. chauvinistic   b. pandemonium   c. panorama

_____ 3. An army general is skilled in _____ activities.

      a. quixotic   b. psyche   c. martial

_____ 4. There was no order, and things were in a state of _____.

      a. boycott   b. maverick   c. pandemonium

_____ 5. His _____ included a journey to many countries.

      a. psychosomatic   b. odyssey   c. quixotic

_____ 6. The people decided to _____ the store.

      a. psyche   b. boycott   c. maverick

_____ 7. The _____ was always rebelling against the orders of his superiors.

      a. quixotic   b. gargantuan   c. maverick

_____ 8. My _____ was upset when my girlfriend broke up with me.

      a. quixotic   b. martial   c. psyche

CHAPTER 7, PART 1 SUPPLEMENTARY EXERCISE

Write in the letter of the word that best completes each sentence.

_____ 1. A professor of great _____ is well-regarded at the university.

   a. tenable   b. eject   c. stature

_____ 2. People were asked to _____ from eating in the theater.

   a. status quo   b. abstain   c. dejected

_____ 3. My _____ friend would never desert me.

   a. conducive   b. abstain   c. staunch

_____ 4. People who do not like change try to maintain the _____.

   a. deduction   b. status quo   c. tenacious

_____ 5. The scientist was able to make a(n) _____ from evidence.

   a. eject   b. deduction   c. abduction

_____ 6. Clean air is _____ to health.

   a. dejected   b. conducive   c. status quo

_____ 7. The _____ crab held on to the swimmer's toe.

   a. eject   b. tenacious   c. tenable

_____ 8. No one believes that the silly theory is _____.

   a. abduction   b. eject   c. tenable

CHAPTER 7, PART 2 SUPPLEMENTARY EXERCISE

Write in the letter of the word that best completes each sentence.

_____ 1. The _____ woman tried to find her child.

      a. circumvent   b. distraught   c. extract

_____ 2. The government wanted to _____ the power of the evil official.

      a. inadvertently   b. perverse   c. circumscribe

_____ 3. The _____ child insisted on wearing his clothing backwards.

      a. transitory   b. perverse   c. adversary

_____ 4. The liquid _____ of flowers is often put into perfume.

      a. extract   b. transformation   c. transcend

_____ 5. _____ people guard their privacy.

      a. Circumscribe   b. Circumvent   c. Circumspect

_____ 6. In prison, the villain underwent a _____ into a religious person.

      a. retract   b. distraught   c. transformation

_____ 7. I hope to _____ my hardships and become successful.

      a. transitory   b. transcend   c. transformation

_____ 8. I _____ said something stupid.

      a. inadvertently   b. adversary   c. retract

CHAPTER 8, PART 1 SUPPLEMENTARY EXERCISE

Write in the letter of the word that best completes each sentence.

_____ 1. People _____ that the judge made a good decision.

      a. coherent   b. discord   c. concur

_____ 2. There is a _____ between his honest words and his dishonest actions.

      a. disreputable   b. disparity   c. communal

_____ 3. The _____ of the opera told us the plot in three paragraphs.

      a. syndrome   b. collaborate   c. synopsis

_____ 4. The play was a _____ of three other plays.

      a. discord   b. synthesis   c. collaborate

_____ 5. A public place is _____ property.

      a. discord   b. disparity   c. communal

_____ 6. The two authors decided to _____ on a book.

      a. contemporary   b. collaborate   c. coherent

_____ 7. The _____ mayor was suspected of taking bribes.

      a. discord   b. compatible   c. disreputable

_____ 8. There was _____ in the fighting group.

      a. discord   b. concur   c. disreputable

CHAPTER 8, PART 2 SUPPLEMENTARY EXERCISE

Write in the letter of the word that best completes each sentence.

_____ 1. Many people are expected to _____ at the rock concert.

      a. sparse   b. congregate   c. cliché

_____ 2. Many plants _____ their seeds into the air.

      a. cuisine   b. segregate   c. disperse

_____ 3. The _____ man had many followers.

      a. nadir   b. intersperse   c. charismatic

_____ 4. After losing the war, the country was at the _____ of its fortunes.

      a. zenith   b. nadir   c. cuisine

_____ 5. I love to eat Pakistani _____.

      a. sparse   b. gregarious   c. cuisine

_____ 6. Farmers often _____ male and female chickens when they hatch.

      a. gregarious   b. sparse   c. segregate

_____ 7. The phrase "good as gold" has become a _____.

      a. zenith   b. disperse   c. cliché

_____ 8. Vegetation is _____ on the top of very high mountains.

      a. sparse   b. cliché   c. gregarious

CHAPTER 9, PART 1 SUPPLEMENTARY EXERCISE

Write in the letter of the word that best completes each sentence.

_____ 1. We were shocked to learn of the _____ of our friend.

a. trilogy   b. duplicity   c. decimate

_____ 2. Because both parties realized the value of the bill, it had _____ support.

a. monarchy   b. trivial   c. bipartisan

_____ 3. It has been over a _____ since the war ended.

a. trivial   b. monopoly   c. decade

_____ 4. We don't have time to spend on that _____ matter.

a. bipartisan   b. trivial   c. dilemma

_____ 5. The _____ student spoke both English and Spanish.

a. bilingual   b. bipartisan   c. dilemma

_____ 6. Since everyone agreed, there was _____ of opinion.

a. unanimity   b. decimate   c. duplicity

_____ 7. War can _____ a country's population.

a. trivial   b. trilogy   c. decimate

_____ 8. She was faced with an unwelcome _____.

a. dilemma   b. decimate   c. unanimity

CHAPTER 9, PART 2 SUPPLEMENTARY EXERCISE

Write in the letter of the word that best completes each sentence.

_____ 1. The Egyptian pyramids are structures of great _____.

  a. metric   b. magnitude   c. magnanimous

_____ 2. I felt _____ about going and did not make up my mind until the last minute.

  a. centennial   b. perennial   c. ambivalence

_____ 3. The _____ of the organization show that its meetings started in 1893.

  a. annals   b. perennial   c. integrity

_____ 4. A minister or preacher is usually a person of _____.

  a. magnanimous   b. ambiguous   c. integrity

_____ 5. In Canada, people use the _____ system of measurement.

  a. annals   b. metric   c. magnitude

_____ 6. Your statement is _____; please clarify it.

  a. magnanimous   b. symmetrical   c. ambiguous

_____ 7. After many years in an attic, newspapers will _____ into dust.

  a. disintegrate   b. perennial   c. magnitude

_____ 8. Mrs. Levy suffered from _____ back pains.

  a. disintegrate   b. ambivalence   c. perennial

CHAPTER 10, PART 1 SUPPLEMENTARY EXERCISE

Write in the letter of the word that best completes each sentence.

_____ 1. Scientists _____ the results of experiments by repeating them.

   a. fidelity   b. veritable   c. verify

_____ 2. The _____ agent handled the company's bank account.

   a. acrophobia   b. credibility   c. fiduciary

_____ 3. The man's _____ prevented him from being comfortable with foreigners.

   a. xenophobia   b. claustrophobia   c. acrophobia

_____ 4. The sergeant lost patience with the _____ soldier.

   a. defiant   b. fidelity   c. veracity

_____ 5. We expressed _____ when told that the circus had a dog that could talk.

   a. credibility   b. incredulity   c. xenophobia

_____ 6. The child's _____ to her parents was wonderful to see.

   a. fidelity   b. veritable   c. verify

_____ 7. The gentle snow soon became a _____ blizzard.

   a. defiant   b. veritable   c. credibility

_____ 8. The _____ of many religions includes loving one's neighbor.

   a. fidelity   b. creed   c. claustrophobia

CHAPTER 10, PART 2 SUPPLEMENTARY EXERCISE

Write in the letter of the word or phrase that best completes each sentence.

_____ 1. When the tennis player lost the first four points to her opponent, she felt she was _____.

      a. destitute   b. behind the eight ball   c. tongue-in-cheek

_____ 2. If you _____ from proper procedure, your results may not be reliable.

      a. give carte blanche   b. deviate   c. leave no stone unturned

_____ 3. The _____ meeting included members of all faiths.

      a. nonchalant   b. destitute   c. nondenominational

_____ 4. Nancy was surprised when others took her _____ comments seriously.

      a. star-crossed   b. nondenominational   c. tongue-in-cheek

_____ 5. I would _____ in an effort to find a lost family member.

      a. give carte blanche   b. leave no stone unturned   c. hold out an olive branch

_____ 6. His _____ attitude showed that he didn't care.

      a. nonchalant   b. delude   c. deviate

_____ 7. His _____ life was filled with disaster.

      a. nonchalant   b. star-crossed   c. behind the eight ball

_____ 8. The president _____ to the vice president to make his own decisions.

      a. gave carte blanche   b. left no stone unturned   c. held out an olive branch

CHAPTER 11, PART 1 SUPPLEMENTARY EXERCISE

Write in the letter of the word that best completes each sentence.

_____ 1. He lost his _____ sense as a result of the explosion in the factory.

         a. inaudible   b. pathology   c. auditory

_____ 2. The sick child looked _____.

         a. pathetic   b. expedite   c. introspection

_____ 3. We would like to _____ this work so that we meet our deadlines.

         a. impede   b. expedite   c. pedigree

_____ 4. The large gorilla was especially _____ because he was surrounded by small animals.

         a. inaudible   b. pathetic   c. conspicuous

_____ 5. Having had polio, I have _____ for other people who suffer from the disease.

         a. audit   b. empathy   c. introspection

_____ 6. Good grades in college classes are a(n) _____ sign for one's later career.

         a. pedigree   b. auspicious   c. expedite

_____ 7. Even during a busy day, Alice sets aside some quiet time for _____.

         a. pathology   b. introspection   c. auditory

_____ 8. The soft beep was _____ to us.

         a. inaudible   b. empathy   c. pedigree

CHAPTER 11, PART 2 SUPPLEMENTARY EXERCISE

Write in the letter of the word that best completes each sentence.

_____ 1. When the government lost control, _____ resulted.

   a. symbiotic   b. malady   c. anarchy

_____ 2. There was a(n) _____ relationship between the parasite and its host.

   a. malpractice   b. symbiotic   c. apathy

_____ 3. His friend appreciated the _____ advice on her term paper.

   a. biopsy   b. beneficial   c. malevolent

_____ 4. The depressed patient displayed _____ about everything.

   a. malady   b. apathy   c. biodegradable

_____ 5. Some movie stars say they want to be _____, but I think they would be upset if no one knew who they were.

   a. apathy   b. malady   c. anonymous

_____ 6. The careless doctor was accused of _____.

   a. malpractice   b. benign   c. malevolent

_____ 7. The _____ revealed that the skin around the tumor should be removed.

   a. malady   b. benign   c. biopsy

_____ 8. People feared the _____ ruler.

   a. biodegradable   b. beneficial   c. malevolent

CHAPTER 12, PART 1 SUPPLEMENTARY EXERCISE

Write in the letter of the word that best completes each sentence.

_____ 1. The actor recited a ten-minute _____.

    a. monologue   b. colloquial   c. advocate

_____ 2. We want to protect the _____ of our lakes and streams.

    a. dictator   b. edict   c. ecology

_____ 3. It is rude to _____ people constantly.

    a. prologue   b. advocate   c. contradict

_____ 4. Most experts in medicine _____ that people should not smoke.

    a. advocate   b. revoke   c. contradict

_____ 5. When speaking with family members, we use a(n) _____ style.

    a. dictator   b. edict   c. colloquial

_____ 6. Cloudy weather is often a(n) _____ to rain or snow.

    a. contradict   b. vociferous   c. prologue

_____ 7. If you disobey rules, your parents may _____ your privileges.

    a. edict   b. invoke   c. revoke

_____ 8. The _____ chairperson did most of the talking.

    a. prologue   b. loquacious   c. contradict

CHAPTER 12, PART 2 SUPPLEMENTARY EXERCISE

Write in the letter of the word that best completes each sentence.

_____ 1. The expression "A stitch in time saves nine" is a(n) _____ .

        a. manuscript   b. effect   c. epigram

_____ 2. If you frown, you _____ that you are unhappy.

        a. infer   b. imply   c. conscious

_____ 3. Using a tape recorder, we were able to _____ every word of the meeting into writing.

        a. demographic   b. conscience   c. transcribe

_____ 4. My _____ will not allow me to cheat on tests.

        a. conscience   b. conscious   c. effect

_____ 5. The _____ material helped students to learn more effectively.

        a. imply   b. graphic   c. affect

_____ 6. The state of our minds will often _____ the quality of our work.

        a. effect   b. imply   c. affect

_____ 7. The _____ was 300 pages long.

        a. epigram   b. inscription   c. manuscript

_____ 8. The _____ survey revealed that 10 percent of citizens live in poverty.

        a. transcribe   b. conscious   c. demographic

PASSAGES

CHAPTER 1, PART 1 SUPPLEMENTARY EXERCISE

Complete each blank with the word that fits best. You may need to capitalize a word when you put it into a sentence. Use each choice only once.

adroit	capricious	gullible
aficionados	cosmopolitan	hypocritical
altruistic	disdain	intrepid
ascetic	fraternal	venerable

(1) _____ of baseball know that top players must work hard. Although no

one expects a player to be a(n) (2) _____ with no fun in his life, players must

have the discipline to practice regularly. After all, no matter what a player's position is, he must be

(3) _____ at handling the ball. If he fumbles too often, he will soon be out of a

job. The owners of ball clubs are not in a(n) (4) _____ business. They are out to

make money, and they cannot afford to keep a bad player.

Baseball players and owners also must be careful to be honest, for the game has had its scandals. In

1919 a few members of the White Sox, a Chicago team, may have decided to make money by intentionally

losing a game. The (5) _____ players appeared to be playing to win, but they

actually may have been making sure that they would lose. However, baseball officials were not

(6) _____ , and they became suspicious enough to conduct an investigation.

None of the players was found guilty. However, after the incident, people started to call the team the

"Black Sox," a term of (7) _____ .

Fortunately, baseball has produced far more heroes than scandals. Men like Babe Ruth and Jackie

Robinson are symbols of talent and hard work. The great Ruth, who played in the 1930s and 1940s, was

one of the best home-run hitters of all time. Ruth was a(n) (8) _____ person who

would do crazy stunts or suddenly change his mind about something for no reason. Jackie Robinson, the

first black person to play in all-white major-league baseball, was (9) _____ in his

courage to face hostile crowds. He combined the talent of a great ball player with a very stable personality.

Because it is well over a century old, baseball holds a(n) (10) _____ position

in the world of sports. Basketball and hockey are examples of newer sports.

Name _____   Date _____

CHAPTER 1, PART 2 SUPPLEMENTARY EXERCISE

Complete each blank with the word that fits best. You may need to capitalize a word when you put it into a sentence. Use each choice only once.

affluent	candid	gauche
alien	dogmatic	novices
amicable	exuberance	renegade
astute	frugal	stoic

I vividly remember my one visit to an expensive French restaurant. Because the prices of this

restaurant were so high, only (1) _____ people could afford it regularly.

However, my girlfriend longed to go, and I wanted to please her. So despite the fact that I am usually

(2) _____, I decided to spend the money. As we entered, the

(3) _____ waiter instantly realized that I was a newcomer. He was

(4) _____, and his friendliness made me feel more comfortable. If he had been

rude, I probably would have left immediately.

Even with the waiter's friendliness, the restaurant seemed (5) _____ to me,

for I had never been in such a fancy place. I felt (6) _____ because I didn't know

how to order or how to use all of the silverware. Unlike me, most of the other diners looked like people

who often ate out at fancy places. After a while, I began to feel more comfortable.

My girlfriend then did something that really embarrassed me. In her

(7) _____ over the delicious taste of the food, she shouted, "Wow, that's great!"

so loudly that everyone could hear. All the sophisticated diners turned around to see who was making so

much noise. Clearly, they knew we were (8) _____ who were not experienced at

eating in fancy restaurants. Although he was probably embarrassed by our outburst, the

(9) _____ waiter displayed no emotion as he answered, "Thank you for your

(10) _____ opinion, madam."

CHAPTER 2, PART 1 SUPPLEMENTARY EXERCISE

Complete each blank with the word that fits best. You may need to capitalize a word when you put it into a sentence. Use each choice only once.

accord	catastrophic	entrepreneurs
attrition	consumers	intervene
bureaucracy	corroborate	media
cartel	diplomacy	pacified

Few nations choose to go to war, for war is a hardship for any nation. Nations involved in a dispute

usually try to reach a(n) (1) _____ without fighting and to settle their differences

by (2) _____. Occasionally, however, a nation feels it must go to war to

defend itself or to seek revenge for a wrong that has been done to it. At other times, nations

(3) _____ to help troubled allies.

Citizens of a nation at war lead difficult lives. Often, store shelves are empty, and

(4) _____ cannot purchase such necessary items as food and clothing. During

wartime, people must make sacrifices. (5) _____ must use their businesses to

manufacture products that help the war effort. Developed nations as well as other countries find that war is

a disaster for their economies.

Nations at war may lose large numbers of their soldiers. Some fall in battle, and others are lost to

gradual (6) _____ from sickness and other problems. Many people are now

aware of the suffering from war because it is covered in the (7) _____. Since

radio and television were invented, reporters have played an important role in telling people back home

what is happening at the battlefront. Eyewitnesses (8) _____ these horrors.

War is devastating even for a victorious nation, but it is usually (9) _____

for the loser. If a nation loses a war, its people must bow to the will of the victors. For all these reasons,

people hope that, in the future, all hostile nations in the world will be (10) _____,

and war will end.

CHAPTER 2, PART 2 SUPPLEMENTARY EXERCISE

Complete each blank with the word that fits best. You may need to capitalize a word when you put it into a sentence. Use each choice only once.

apprehend	epitome	radically
chaotic	liberalize	reactionary
conserve	ludicrous	supplanted
deferred	ominous	thrive

People have always dreamed about a perfect society. Many have had visions of a society that would be

(1) _____ different from their own. The ancient Greek philosopher Plato wrote of

a world in which everything would be in perfect order and things would never be

(2) _____. The city described in his *Republic* was the

(3) _____ of a state ruled by reason. In Plato's republic, free will was to be

(4) _____ by obedience to wise men called "philosopher kings." Since these

rulers would be able to (5) _____ best the nature of justice, they would be the

wisest rulers. When people were governed by wisdom, Plato thought, they would

(6) _____ and prosper.

In the 1500s, Sir Thomas More wrote about a perfect place called Utopia (which means "nowhere"). In

this state, all the people would share all the property. Thus, everyone would work for the common good and

would be motivated to (7) _____ the commonwealth. Although some people

thought that More's ideas were so silly that they were (8) _____ , others thought

that they would work.

Plato's and More's ideas were never tested. More recently, people have actually tried to live in ideal

communities. Many of these communities had a(n) (9) _____ philosophy, and

people in them refused to use modern inventions and conveniences. Although a few of these communities

succeeded, many others have failed. Because of these failures, many people have concluded that the

realization of a perfect society may have to be (10) _____ until far into the

future.

CHAPTER 3, PART 1 SUPPLEMENTARY EXERCISE

Complete each blank with the word that fits best. You may need to capitalize a word when you put it into a sentence. Use each choice only once.

bland	confrontation	emulate
boisterous	dynamic	enigmatic
clarify	elated	skeptical
concise	emphatically	thwart

Students should feel comfortable asking a professor about any point in a lecture that seems

(1) _____ to them. Professors usually welcome the opportunity to

(2) _____ points that students do not understand. Most professors

(3) _____ state that they want their students to understand everything. Professors

may actually be (4) _____ that students are showing a sincere interest in the

subject. A question from a student may often give a professor the opportunity to summarize an important

idea in a(n) (5) _____ form that students will understand immediately.

Of course, certain types of student behavior are not welcome in the classroom. Everyone has seen

(6) _____ students who make so much noise that the professor cannot be heard.

This type of disorder can (7) _____ all learning, producing a situation in which

students cannot acquire knowledge.

On the other hand, many professors enjoy comments from (8) _____

students who are thoughtful enough not to believe everything that they hear. The discussion between a

professor and a challenging student often livens up a class and keeps it from becoming

(9) _____ and dull. Students should not be afraid that their questions will be seen

as attempts to have a(n) (10) _____ with the professor.

CHAPTER 3, PART 2 SUPPLEMENTARY EXERCISE

Complete each blank with the word that fits best. You may need to capitalize a word when you put it into a sentence. Use each choice only once.

appalled	condemned	flaunt
articulated	contemplate	harassing
belligerent	contended	prohibited
chagrined	eliciting	undermine

Recently I spent a day observing cases in court, and I learned that a judge may be called on to make

many types of decisions. First, I witnessed a group of teenagers who were being tried for

(1) _____ young children by stealing their money every day on the way to

school. The judge was (2) _____ that such little children should be victims. She

(3) _____ the actions of the teenagers and set a harsh punishment. One of the

teenagers became (4) _____ and actually tried to start a fight.

Next, there was a case of slander, in which one businessman (5) _____ that

another was trying to (6) _____ his reputation by telling lies about him.

There were many complex legal points in this case, and the judge called a recess so that she could have

some time to (7) _____ them.

Finally, there was a case of drunken driving. The judge took away the man's license and

(8) _____ him from driving for a year. The judge asked him to think of the

consequences before drinking and driving again.

I was impressed by the judge's ability to handle different types of cases. Although she didn't

(9) _____ her knowledge, it was clear that she had a deep understanding of the

law. She (10) _____ this understanding clearly, giving good reasons for each of

her decisions.

CHAPTER 4, PART 1 SUPPLEMENTARY EXERCISE

Complete each blank with the word that fits best. You may need to capitalize a word when you put it into a sentence. Use each choice only once.

accolades	cryptic	meticulous
augment	indulged	obsolete
chivalry	jeopardized	perpetually
complacent	mandatory	zeal

In his long life as a war correspondent, writer, and politician, Winston Churchill (1874–1965)

witnessed many changes. He watched as the horse and buggy became (1) _____

and were replaced by the car. He saw gaslight give way to electricity. He saw the British Empire

(2) _____ its territories, and then he watched as the empire dissolved.

Churchill's mother was American; his father had been an ambitious politician whose career ended

when he became ill. From an early age, Churchill showed ambition and energy. He first became famous

when he covered the Boer War for a London newspaper. In his (3) _____ to cover each event,

he often found himself in dangerous situations. At times he (4) _____ his life, risking death to

get a story for his newspaper.

Churchill then went into politics, overseeing the British Navy during World War I. The navy had an

excellent reputation, but Churchill did not want its officers to become (5) _____. He urged

the navy to experiment with new inventions, such as the airplane. He also urged navy personnel to take

(6) _____ care of equipment, so that it would always be ready if it were needed suddenly.

Not everyone liked Churchill. He changed political parties twice during his career, causing many

politicians to distrust him. At times his humorous insults, particularly those directed at ladies, caused others

to accuse him of a lack of (7) _____. He liked many luxuries, and

(8) _____ himself by spending so much money on clothes that his wife sometimes

complained. Because he loved luxury, he was (9) _____ short of money.

The height of Churchill's career came when he served as prime minister during World War II. In the

early days of the war, Britain fought against overwhelming odds. Churchill's wonderful speeches inspired

the nation to continue fighting. For this great contribution, Churchill received many

(10) _____ from his own country and from others.

CHAPTER 4, PART 2 SUPPLEMENTARY EXERCISE

Complete each blank with the word that fits best. You may need to capitalize a word when you put it into a sentence. Use each choice only once.

accelerate	cultivation	pinnacle
adulated	euphemism	procrastinate
chronological	mammoth	successive
copious	mitigate	withstand

Compared to the earth, the sun is of (1) _____ size. Life on earth is

dependent on this huge star. The sun supplies the energy necessary for life. Without the sun, there

could be no (2) _____ of crops. Many ancient cultures

(3) _____ and worshiped the sun, thinking that it must be a god or goddess.

Holidays were dedicated to the sun.

Most people love to sit in the sun and absorb its rays, and at one time a suntan was considered healthy.

Recently, however, doctors have discovered that sitting in the sun can be dangerous. Indeed, they say that

the term *suntan* is really a(n) (4) _____ for a burn. For, as the skin tans, it is

experiencing a burning reaction. People who are always out in the sun have an increased risk of skin

cancer. It is particularly hard for people with fair skin to (5) _____ the harmful

effects of the sun. Doctors warn such people not to sit in the sun for more than twenty

(6) _____ minutes. Whether your skin is fair or dark, doctors suggest that you

should (7) _____ the harmful effects of the sun by wearing a sunscreen lotion.

Doctors advise not to (8) _____ in putting on sunscreen, but to make sure you are

protected from the first moments your skin is exposed to the sun's rays. Sun can also

(9) _____ the aging process of your skin and make you look older sooner.

At one time, (10) _____ amounts of sunlight were thought to be healthy, and

people were advised to get plenty of sunlight. Now doctors realize that exposure to the sun can harm you.

CHAPTER 5, PART 1 SUPPLEMENTARY EXERCISE

Complete each blank with the word that fits best. You may need to capitalize a word when you put it into a sentence. Use each choice only once.

antidote	equitable	reverted
antipathy	equivocal	subconscious
antithetical	reconcile	subdue
equilibrium	revelation	subordinates

Although many young people in the United States and Canada have lived through hard economic times, few have lived through a full depression. The Great Depression of the 1930s came as a shock because it was completely (1) _____ to the prosperity of the 1920s. It started with the stock market crash of 1929. After this disaster, the economy became unbalanced. When the economy lost its (2) _____, millions of people lost their jobs. Many people who had once been rich experienced the unwelcome (3) _____ of what it was like to live in poverty.

The effects of the Depression were not (4) _____ and did not affect everyone alike. Women and minorities suffered more than the rest of the population. Even those who managed to find jobs often suffered a reduction of salary or position. During the Depression, many people who had been self-employed found that they had to (5) _____ themselves to taking low-level jobs. In contrast, during this time, many movies depicted rich people living in luxury. Perhaps this satisfied (6) _____ desires on the part of citizens who were struggling to make a living.

The Republican president Herbert Hoover did not react quickly to the crisis, and the feelings of many people toward him changed from admiration to (7) _____. Consequently, the Democratic candidate, Franklin D. Roosevelt, was elected president in 1932. Roosevelt and his (8) _____ tried to create jobs through public works projects. These projects created some jobs, but the results were (9) _____ , and many believe that Roosevelt's programs actually did little for the economy. However, Roosevelt's efforts made him very popular. Many economists now believe that after a slight upswing due to New Deal programs, the economy (10) _____ to its previous low level until the Depression ended in the 1940s, after World War II.

CHAPTER 5, PART 2 SUPPLEMENTARY EXERCISE

Complete each blank with the word that fits best. You may need to capitalize a word when you put it into a sentence. Use each choice only once.

autobiographical   exorbitant   incongruous
autocratic   exploit   ingenious
autonomous   extricate   interminably
eccentricities   impartial   invariably

Robots are being used in industry to perform tasks that human beings find dull and to carry out other

specialized tasks. Although the initial cost of building them can be (1) _____, the

owners often save money in the long run. A human being tires after performing a task on an assembly line

for several hours, but a robot can perform a task (2) _____ . There is no change

in the work done by a robot, and it (3) _____ produces the same product. Robots

have no (4) _____ wills, and they never ask why. Finally, of course, robots have

no human (5) _____, the surprising differences that make human beings so

interesting. Not surprisingly, many businesses are beginning to (6) _____ the

new advances in robot technology by making and using robots.

Robots have some surprising uses. Recently a(n) (7) _____ scientist built a

robot that can locate a brain tumor in a patient's head and determine the best place to do surgery. Thus, the

use of a robot can (8) _____ the surgeon from the difficulty of doing surgery

based on guesses.

Of course, robots have some bad features. Many workers are afraid that they will be replaced by robots

and left jobless. However, because robots cannot think, human employees will always be needed.

(9) _____ observers say that robots probably benefit human beings because they

expand industry and, therefore, create more jobs. Thus, the use of robots is not

(10) _____ with employment for humans.

CHAPTER 6, PART 1 SUPPLEMENTARY EXERCISE

Complete each blank with the word that fits best. You may need to capitalize a word when you put it into a sentence. Use each choice only once.

anthropological	misanthropic	renown
congenital	nominal	viable
genesis	philanthropist	vitally
genocide	pseudonym	vivacious

The children's book *Alice in Wonderland* is one of the most popular stories of all time. It was written

by an Oxford mathematician, Charles Dodgson, who used the (1) _____ "Lewis

Carroll." Under this name, the shy Dodgson became an author of great (2) _____.

The book had its (3) _____ in a story told to a child, Alice Liddell. The

(4) _____ and cheerful child had charmed Dodgson.

The story tells how Alice's adventures start when she falls down a hole chasing a rabbit. The rabbit is

carrying a watch and mumbling, "I shall be too late."

After she falls underground, Alice eats various items of food that make her grow larger or smaller. She

meets the Cheshire Cat, who has a(n) (5) _____ smile that he seems to have been

born with. She also meets the (6) _____ Queen of Hearts, who is eager to

sentence people to death, even if they haven't been found guilty of a crime.

A friend convinced Dodgson that his manuscript would be a(n) (7) _____

publication. Dodgson arranged for the artist John Tenniel to draw the illustrations, and the book was

published. Many people consider the pictures to be (8) _____ important to its

charm.

Over one hundred years later, *Alice in Wonderland* remains a popular book. In Dodgson's day, the

book sold for only a(n) (9) _____ amount. But today, the value of early editions

has increased dramatically. In fact, any person who bought a first edition and donated it to a library would

now be considered a(n) (10) _____ who had made a generous gift.

CHAPTER 6, PART 2 SUPPLEMENTARY EXERCISE

Complete each blank with the word that fits best. You may need to capitalize a word when you put it into a sentence. Use each choice only once.

boycott	maverick	psyche
chauvinistic	odyssey	psychosomatic
gargantuan	pandemonium	quixotic
martial	panorama	spartan

Peter the Great (1672–1725) was one of the most energetic rulers of Russia. Because his father died when Peter was young, his throne was in danger. In fact, the palace was invaded during his childhood, and several of Peter's relatives died in the (1) _____ before the invaders left and order was restored. This invasion must have deeply troubled Peter's (2) _____, for he was careful never to lose control of any situation again. Perhaps his ability to control situations was aided by his physical tallness. Well over six feet tall, Peter must have seemed (3) _____ to the shorter people of his age.

Peter was a great (4) _____ leader who excelled in the art of warfare. He defeated the cruel enemy tribes who had attacked Russia and sold people into slavery. Peter enjoyed going to war even though his (5) _____ existence on the battlefield contrasted sharply with the luxurious life he lived in the palace.

Unfortunately, Peter also fought with his son, a(n) (6) _____ who refused to follow his father's orders. The son was a troubled person who suffered from many (7) _____ illnesses. Their quarrels led to the son's death.

Peter was interested in establishing more ties with other countries. A youthful (8) _____ to Europe had convinced him that the continent was advanced in many ways. His view of Russia was not (9) _____ and he felt that European cultures could offer many advantages to his country. He built the city of St. Petersburg on the western border of Russia. The city was difficult and expensive to construct because most of it was built on marshes. Many thought that Peter's desire to build the city was simply a(n) (10) _____ dream and could never be accomplished. However, the city was completed and remains, even today, one of the most beautiful in the world.

Name _____   Date _____

CHAPTER 7, PART 1 SUPPLEMENTARY EXERCISE

Complete each blank with the word that fits best. You may need to capitalize a word when you put it into a sentence. Use each choice only once.

abducted	dejected	status quo
abstain	ejected	staunch
conducive	jettison	tenable
deduction	stature	tenacious

Sherlock Holmes is the fictional detective created by Sir Arthur Conan Doyle. Holmes is a master of

(1) _____ who, using only a few clues, can determine how a crime took place.

Once on a case, Holmes is (2) _____ and will not give it up until justice has been

done. Holmes receives the assistance of his (3) _____ and loyal friend, Dr.

Watson. Although Dr. Watson tries to solve the crimes, he is not as smart as Holmes, and his theories are

never quite (4) _____.

Holmes has a very private personality. He often sits in one position for hours, considering the evidence

in a case. He also finds that playing the violin is an activity (5) _____ to thinking.

Holmes has some bad habits, such as using drugs, but he tries to (6) _____ from

them while he is working on a case. Holmes often gets depressed, and his friend Watson, who is always

unhappy to see him (7) _____, tries to cheer him up.

Holmes has solved many murders. He has rescued (8) _____ women and

restored them to their families. Perhaps his most famous case is "The Hound of the Baskervilles," in which

a fierce beast terrorizes a lonely farm country.

Holmes is so brilliant that he usually solves a crime before the police do. This upsets people who

believe in the (9) _____ and like to think that law officers are the best people to

solve crimes.

The fictional detective Holmes has achieved such fame and (10) _____

through the stories he appears in that some have come to believe that he is real. In fact, however, he is

merely the creation of Conan Doyle.

CHAPTER 7, PART 2 SUPPLEMENTARY EXERCISE

Complete each blank with the word that fits best. You may need to capitalize a word when you put it into a sentence. Use each choice only once.

adversary	distraught	retract
circumscribing	extracting	transcend
circumspect	inadvertently	transform
circumvent	perverse	transitory

Specialists in sports psychology can help players win games and become popular with fans. For

example, to win against a tough (1) _____, a professional tennis player must

avoid getting upset. If a player becomes (2) _____ because he is behind in a

game, he will probably never catch up. In such a situation, a player must

(3) _____ his or her negative emotions and simply concentrate on the game.

Tennis fans like to see players maintain control of their tempers. Even a(n)

(4) _____ display of anger will annoy onlookers. Sometimes, players can

(5) _____ create problems for themselves, for referees can punish or expel

players who are temperamental.

A tennis player is expected to show good sportsmanship. One tennis player became unpopular because

he was not gracious about a championship that he had won. The public felt that his lack of politeness was

(6) _____ , and critical stories appeared about him in the newspapers. Other

players have made foolish remarks, which they later had to (7) _____. Still others

have not been (8) _____ in their private lives and have caused scandals.

To (9) _____ such difficulties, a player may seek the advice of a sports

psychologist. This expert can show a temperamental player how to control emotions and be more gracious

to the public. A sports psychologist cannot completely (10) _____ a player's

character but can help players avoid many problems.

CHAPTER 8, PART 1 SUPPLEMENTARY EXERCISE

Complete each blank with the word that fits best. You may need to capitalize a word when you put it into a sentence. Use each choice only once.

coherent	concur	disreputable
collaborated	contemporary	syndrome
commune	discord	synopsize
compatible	disparity	synthesis

The advice columns that appear in many newspapers are popular daily reading. These columns often

contain questions and answers that touch on (1) _____ problems of love,

manners, and family living in the modern world. For example, a woman might write because she finds that

she and her husband are not (2) _____. Her husband likes to be alone, but she is a

person who likes large parties. Not surprisingly, this causes (3) _____ in the

marriage. The advice columnist gives her a possible solution, and the many readers of the column can see

whether or not they (4) _____ with the advice.

Recently, a woman wrote complaining that she was bothered by the (5) _____

between her relatives' wealth and her poverty. Another wrote because she wanted to know how to

discourage a (6) _____ man who had been asking her out on dates. These people

had to (7) _____ the problems of many months into a letter of only a few

paragraphs. The letters had to be (8) _____ enough to be easily understood.

People who write advice columns often seek the opinions of doctors and lawyers who are experts in a

certain field. In a recent column, an advice columnist (9) _____ with a well-

known doctor to discuss the problems of cancer. The column was a (10) _____, a

combination of the views of the columnist and the doctor.

CHAPTER 8, PART 2 SUPPLEMENTARY EXERCISE

Complete each blank with the word that fits best. You may need to capitalize a word when you put it into a sentence. Use each choice only once.

bravado	cuisines	nadir
charismatic	dispersed	segregated
cliché	gregarious	sparsity
congregations	interspersed	zenith

The Crusades, a series of European wars to capture and hold Jerusalem, took place from approximately

1100 to 1300. The Crusades were considered holy wars, and priests often urged members of their

(1) _____ to go. Occasionally, a(n) (2) _____ leader

would inspire several thousand people to follow him. The (3) _____ of the

movement was when Jerusalem was captured by the Europeans.

Most of the Crusades, however, ended in failure. For example, Richard the Lion-Hearted, king of

England, reached the (4) _____ of his career when he was captured by a German

prince on his way home from the Crusades. Richard tried to threaten his captors, but, realizing that his

threats were only (5) _____ , they were not impressed. He was not released until

the English people had raised a large ransom.

Soldiers and common people had many adventures on the Crusades. They often were

(6) _____ and made friends as they traveled. Prayers and religious services were

(7) _____ with parties and social gatherings. During the Crusades in Arab lands,

Europeans discovered tangerines, apricots, coffee, and many other products of foreign cultures that

enlivened their (8) _____ .

However, there also was hardship. When crusaders crossed the deserts, the

(9) _____ of crops caused starvation, and there was much illness. Often the

groups were so disorganized that they never reached Jerusalem. In that situation, the crowds of people

simply (10) _____ and tried to find their way back home, one by one.

CHAPTER 9, PART 1 SUPPLEMENTARY EXERCISE

Complete each blank with the word that fits best. You may need to capitalize a word when you put it into a sentence. Use each choice only once.

bilingual	dilemma	trilogy
bipartisan	duplicity	trivial
decade	monarchy	unanimity
decimate	monopoly	unilateral

The American Revolution lasted from 1775 to 1783, two years less than a(n)

(1) _____ . It had many causes. Some American traders resented the

(2) _____ that British merchants had on trade. Other colonists were angered by

the fact that the English Parliament imposed taxes on the colonists in a(n)

(3) _____ fashion, without allowing the colonists a voice in the taxing decisions.

However, there was no (4) _____ of opinion about the British. While some

people were angry with them, other Americans liked British rule and did not favor the Revolution. People

with this opinion usually faced a(n) (5) _____ . Either they had to leave the

colonies, or they risked the hatred of their neighbors.

The American Revolution was the only time in history when several separate colonies joined together

to rebel against their ruler. Although George Washington, whom the colonists elected as their leader, was

southern, he had (6) _____ support, from both northern and southern colonies.

Some German soldiers also fought beside the Americans. Often (7) _____ people

who could speak both German and English were used to command these troops.

At first, the British thought that it would be a(n) (8) _____ matter to defeat

the Americans. However, the Americans were skilled in fighting in the countryside, and they often hid in

the woods to shoot at the British as they stood in open fields. These tactics enabled the Americans to

(9) _____ the British troops.

There were some traitors on both sides. The famous American soldier Benedict Arnold showed his

(10) _____ when he tried to let the British capture West Point. Fortunately,

Arnold's plan was discovered.

Name _____ Date _____

CHAPTER 9, PART 2 SUPPLEMENTARY EXERCISE

Complete each blank with the word that fits best. You may need to capitalize a word when you put it into a sentence. Use each choice only once.

ambiguous   centigrade   magnitude
ambivalent   disintegrated   metric
annals   integrity   perennial
centennial   magnanimous   symmetry

The (1) _____ of history record the greatness of the Roman Empire. At first, Rome was a republic, and there were constant power struggles at home. The (2) _____ lack of peace must have made some citizens long for more stability. When Julius Caesar seized control of Rome, many citizens wondered if he would make himself emperor, and they must have felt (3) _____ about the issue. On the one hand, an emperor might bring more order; on the other hand, he might prove to be a cruel dictator. It seemed that Caesar himself was uncertain. He gave some (4) _____ hints that he might like to be emperor, but he never declared his intentions clearly. Before Caesar could make up his mind, he was assassinated.

Caesar's nephew, Octavian, became the first emperor. Although several members of his family were emperor after him, they failed to establish a dynasty. Some were men of (5) _____, but others plotted to assassinate their enemies. Court life (6) _____ into a series of murders and plots. The Roman Empire was founded in 30 B.C.E.; by 68 C.E., shortly before the (7) _____ of the Empire, the relatives of Octavian and Caesar had lost power. Future emperors were chosen by the army.

In contrast to their chaotic court life, the Romans were excellent administrators. By any standard, the Roman Empire was huge. The Romans did a good job of governing an empire of this (8) _____. When they conquered a country they were (9) _____, usually showing mercy toward the defeated people. They governed wisely and introduced systems of roads, water supply, and postal delivery. Their system of measurement, with 1,000 paces to the mile, was the forerunner of the (10) _____ system.

128 / Part III: Supplementary and Review Exercises   Copyright © Houghton Mifflin Company. All rights reserved.

CHAPTER 10, PART 1 SUPPLEMENTARY EXERCISE

Complete each blank with the word that fits best. You may need to capitalize a word when you put it into a sentence. Use each choice only once.

acrophobic	defiant	veracity
claustrophobic	fidelity	verify
credibility	fiduciary	veritable
creeds	incredulous	xenophobic

Human beings have many different types of beliefs. Most people believe in the

(1) _____ of their fellow human beings and usually assume that they are telling

the truth. Few people try to (2) _____ everything that they are told by others.

People also have social beliefs. Most of us are loyal and supportive of our friends and families and

display (3) _____ toward them even when they are in trouble.

Our entire business system is also based on belief. For example, people deposit money into banks

because they believe that they will be able to withdraw it. Many people were

(4) _____ when banks failed during the Great Depression and could not refund

money. In the same way, people believe that their (5) _____ agents, the people to

whom they entrust money, will be honest. Any agent who betrayed such trust would lack

(6) _____ and would soon be out of business.

Most people display belief in the (7) _____ of their religions. However, the

history of religion has also included disagreement. Most new religions were founded by

(8) _____ people who did not believe in an already established religion and

therefore refused to follow it.

People also have personal beliefs that may seem strange to others. For example,

(9) _____ people subconsciously believe that small spaces will harm them. Such

people often break out into a(n) (10) _____ panic when they go into elevators or

closets.

CHAPTER 10, PART 2 SUPPLEMENTARY EXERCISE

Complete each blank with the word or phrase that fits best. You may need to capitalize a word when you put it into a sentence. Use each choice only once.

behind the eight ball	gave carte blanche	nondenominational
delude	held out an olive branch	nondescript
destitute	left no stone unturned	star-crossed
deviated	nonchalant	tongue-in-cheek

We began to feel that our town was simply (1) _____ when we learned that,

for the third time in three years, a hurricane would strike us. At four o'clock in the afternoon, we learned

that the hurricane was expected to strike the next morning. We had expected this one to miss us by more

than 300 miles. However, the hurricane had (2) _____ from its expected course

and now was heading toward us. We (3) _____ to the civil defense authorities to

do anything they could to mitigate the disaster. They realized that they were already

(4) _____, for the late warning had delayed preparations. They

(5) _____ to protect us. They put sandbags on the river banks, tied down loose

objects throughout the town, and got out rescue boats. However, preparations barely got underway before

most of us left town.

But a few people remained behind. Some had managed to (6) _____

themselves into thinking that the weather forecasters were wrong. Their (7) _____

attitudes contrasted sharply with our panic.

The hurricane struck with full force. After it was over, many of us returned to find homes and

businesses gone. Many were left (8) _____ when their property was destroyed.

But there was a bright side to the hurricane, for it united people. Families who had fought for years

suddenly (9) _____ and made peace. Even humor appeared when someone made

the (10) _____ comment that "It certainly was a windy day."

CHAPTER 11, PART 1 SUPPLEMENTARY EXERCISE

Complete each blank with the word that fits best. You may need to capitalize a word when you put it into a sentence. Use each choice only once.

audited	empathic	introspection
auditory	expedite	pathetic
auspicious	impeded	pathology
conspicuous	inaudible	pedigrees

The science of medicine has done much to conquer disease. If we were put back 300 years in time, we would be shocked by how unhealthy people were. Disease played a(n) (1) _____ part in human life. Even members of the nobility were haunted by illness. Their great wealth and

(2) _____ could not protect them from the lack of medical knowledge of their day.

Scientists today feel that some past medical practices were actually harmful. Leeches were used to bleed the sick. Operations were done in unsanitary conditions that (3) _____ recovery rather than aiding it. Dentistry also involved much pain. It is said that dentists once had musicians play so that the screams of their patients would be (4) _____ to others. It is easy for us to feel sorry for those (5) _____ people who were the victims of the lack of medical knowledge.

Modern medicine is much different. Today we know the (6) _____ of many diseases, and we can prevent them. Scarlet fever, a disease that may damage the

(7) _____ nerve and cause deafness, can be treated with antibiotics. Polio and measles can now be prevented through immunization. When surgery is necessary, clean conditions help to avoid infection and to (8) _____ recovery.

There have also been many advances in mental health. The psychiatrist Sigmund Freud used

(9) _____ to analyze his own life and its problems. This led to psychoanalysis, a method now used to treat mental illness.

The lengthening of the average human life span in developed countries is a(n)

(10) _____ sign for developing countries. However, much remains to be accomplished in the health care of poorer nations.

CHAPTER 11, PART 2 SUPPLEMENTARY EXERCISE

Complete each blank with the word that fits best. You may need to capitalize a word when you put it into a sentence. Use each choice only once.

anarchy	beneficial	malady
anonymous	benign	malevolence
apathetic	biodegradable	malpractice
benefactors	biopsy	symbiotic

A person must have many qualities to become a surgeon. First, surgeons must be skillful with their

hands. A clumsy surgeon might make many errors that would cause him or her to be sued for

(1) _____ . A surgeon must also thoroughly understand the patient's

(2) _____ . Operations can be dangerous, and a surgeon must make sure that any

risk is at a minimum and that an operation has a good chance of being (3) _____

to a patient's health.

Surgeons must actually care about their patients. Few patients feel comfortable with a surgeon who

appears to be (4) _____ and uncaring. They may even mistake such an attitude

for (5) _____ and feel that the surgeon wishes them harm. Because of this, most

patients want to talk at length to their surgeons before an operation. Patients would understandably feel fear

if they were operated on by a(n) (6) _____ surgeon whom they had never met

and whose name they might not even know.

Once in the operating room, there are rigid rules that guide procedures. Everything must be under

control, and even the slightest hint of (7) _____ must be avoided. The surgeon is

the boss, and others must obey. During an operation, the surgeon often must take a(n)

(8) _____ of the patient's tissue. This is sent to a laboratory, where a pathologist

determines whether it is (9) _____ or malignant.

Several surgeons have recently pioneered open heart surgery, heart transplants, and the use of artificial

hearts. These surgeons' fame has helped their hospitals to raise money. (10) _____

are often pleased to contribute money to hospitals that are making medical history.

CHAPTER 12, PART 1 SUPPLEMENTARY EXERCISE

Complete each blank with the word that fits best. You may need to capitalize a word when you put it into a sentence. Use each choice only once.

advocate	ecology	monologue
colloquial	edicts	prologue
contradicting	invoke	revoke
dictators	loquacious	vociferate

During the course of history, many rulers have become (1) _____ holding

absolute power. Few people dare to disobey a dictator's (2) _____. He can

(3) _____ any law that he chooses to change. If he wants to deliver a four-hour

(4) _____ to the people, no one will stop him. He can damage the

(5) _____ of a country by encouraging policies that harm air quality and water

purity, and no one will dare to stop this damage.

Often, however, people's behavior is based on fear, for a dictator can (6) _____

his power to control even the smallest deviation in his people's behavior. People who

(7) _____ doing things in a way the dictator disapproves of are persecuted.

(8) _____ something that a dictator has said is also dangerous. Even the slightest

disagreement about his policies may cause a dictator to arrest citizens. People who are insistent enough to

(9) _____ repeatedly against his policies may be killed.

Not surprisingly, most people want to avoid living under a dictator. Maintaining a strong democracy is

the best way to ensure that a dictator will not seize power. The failure of a democracy is often the

(10) _____ to the rule of a dictator.

CHAPTER 12, PART 2 SUPPLEMENTARY EXERCISE

Complete each blank with the word that fits best. You may need to capitalize a word when you put it into a sentence. Use each choice only once.

affected	effect	infer
conscience	epigram	inscriptions
conscious	graphic	manuscript
demographic	implies	transcribed

Before the invention of movable type, making copies of books was a time-consuming and expensive

process. To make another copy of a book, it had to be fully (1) _____ by hand.

Monks spent weeks copying each (2) _____ of a book. The labor involved in

book production (3) _____ the type of book that was produced. Books of long

ago were distinctive and highly artistic products. They were filled with beautiful

(4) _____ work, such as pictures and illustrated letters. They often bore moving

(5) _____ that thanked the people who had made the book's production possible.

The very beauty of these books (6) _____ that people spent much time producing

them.

However, books were very expensive, and few people could buy them. This unavailability of books

had a(n) (7) _____ on education, and few people were taught to read. A(n)

(8) _____ survey of Europe in the 1300s probably would have revealed that less

than 10 percent of people were literate.

In the 1400s, when printed books became available, people slowly became (9) _____

of the value of reading. We can (10) _____ from this that the human desire to do

something can be affected by its usefulness. When there were few books to read, reading was seen as

useless, and few desired to learn the skill. As more books were produced, the skill of reading became more

useful, and more people wanted to master it.

REVIEW EXERCISES

CHAPTERS 1 THROUGH 6 REVIEW EXERCISE

Learning Strategies

A. *Dictionary clues*   Write in the letter of the choice that fits best in each blank. Use each choice only once.

_____ 1. A key is used to find the _____ of a word.

   a. history   b. definition   c. pronunciation   d. connotation

_____ 2. A listing of *n.* and *tr. v.* indicates that the word functions as a _____.

   a. noun and intransitive verb   b. neuter and transitive verb   c. noun and transitive verb
   d. noun and verbal

_____ 3. The different forms of a verb are _____.

   a. listed in a dictionary under separate entries   b. listed in a dictionary under one entry
   c. not listed in a dictionary

B. *Context clues*   Using context clues, make an intelligent guess at the meaning of the underlined word in each sentence.

4. We must <u>persevere</u> and never give up.

   Persevere means _____ .

5. The <u>apogee</u> of his career was when he was elected President of the United States.

   Apogee means _____ .

6. The <u>restive</u> child was unhappy that she had to sit waiting in the car for half an hour.

   Restive means _____ .

7. The <u>tintinnabulation</u> of the bells was heard throughout the town.

   Tintinnabulation means _____ .

8. We were surprised at the man's <u>feral</u> behavior when he gnawed on a piece of meat like a hungry lion.

   Feral means _____ .

9. The strict teacher would tolerate no <u>infractions</u> of rules.

   Infractions means _____ .

10. Because the man was <u>remiss</u> about making his payments for the refrigerator, the store took it away from him.

   Remiss means _____ .

C. *Combining context clues and word elements*   Use your knowledge of context clues and word elements to make an intelligent guess at the meaning of the underlined word in each sentence.

11.   The artist was told to <u>vivify</u> the colors in the painting.

<u>Vivify</u> means _____ .

12.   He was tried for the crime, but the jury <u>exculpated</u> him.

<u>Exculpated</u> means _____ .

13.   People who believe in <u>reincarnation</u> may expect to return to life as a cat or a tree.

<u>Reincarnation</u> means _____ .

14.   The study of <u>psychopathology</u> is one branch of medicine.

<u>Psychopathology</u> means _____ .

15.   He was given a <u>subportion</u> of the prize money.

<u>Subportion</u> means _____ .

Word Element Meanings

Write the letter of its definition beside each word element in the left-hand column. Use each choice only once.

_____ 1. pan-   a. birth

_____ 2. gen   b. under

_____ 3. ex-   c. not

_____ 4. in-   d. against

_____ 5. anti-   e. human being

                                    f. all

                                    g. out

Definitions

Write the letter of its definition by each word in the left-hand column. Use each choice only once.

_____ 1. exorbitant

_____ 2. quixotic

_____ 3. skeptical

_____ 4. cultivate

_____ 5. radical

_____ 6. affluent

_____ 7. cosmopolitan

_____ 8. defer

_____ 9. elated

_____ 10. contemplate

_____ 11. ingenious

_____ 12. vivacious

_____ 13. pandemonium

_____ 14. aficionado

_____ 15. supplant

a. wealthy

b. a fan

c. to grow deliberately

d. to think about

e. to delay

f. very expensive

g. from several parts of the world

h. doubtful

i. helpful

j. to replace

k. lively

l. silly

m. clever

n. very happy

o. disorder

p. favoring great change

q. idealistic but unrealistic

Words in Context

Write beside each sentence number the letter of the word that best completes that sentence. Use each choice only once.

A. a. accord
   b. viable
   c. exploit
   d. stoic

   e. augment
   f. antidote
   g. capricious
   h. adroit

   i. conservative
   j. mitigating
   k. enigma
   l. martial

_____ 1. The _____ attitudes of the country convinced its neighbor that it wanted war.

_____ 2. The computer programmer's _____ mind could easily add several columns of figures.

_____ 3. A(n) _____ person almost never complains.

_____ 4. Because the murder was never solved, the identity of the murderer remains a(n) _____.

_____ 5. The _____ child wanted a different toy every five minutes.

_____ 6. It is wrong to _____ people by underpaying them.

_____ 7. The _____ seed was able to grow into a plant.

_____ 8. Because of _____ circumstances in the crime, the judge reduced the criminal's sentence.

_____ 9. Love can be the _____ to unhappiness.

_____ 10. We reached a(n) _____ that satisfied everyone.

B. a. boycott   e. subdue   i. obsolete
   b. extricate   f. fraternal   j. emulate
   c. appall   g. corroborate   k. impartial
   d. chronological   h. liberal   l. genocide

_____ 11. The unfair employment policies of the store caused a citizens' group to _____ it.

_____ 12. A public official who could not read or write would _____ everybody who cared about education.

_____ 13. The hand-cranked ice-cream maker is now _____.

_____ 14. I would like to _____ myself from this hopeless situation.

_____ 15. The _____ politician favored extending more rights to poor people.

_____ 16. A referee in a wrestling match should be _____.

_____ 17. We must prevent the horrible crime of _____.

_____ 18. I try to _____ my feelings of anger so that I will stay calm.

_____ 19. The student wanted to _____ the teacher he admired.

_____ 20. The two friends had close _____ feelings.

CHAPTERS 7 THROUGH 12 REVIEW EXERCISE

Learning Strategies

A. *Word element meanings*   Write the letter of its definition by each word element in the left-hand column. Use each choice only once.

_____ 1. bi-		a. life
_____ 2. dict-		b. across
_____ 3. bio-		c. together; same
_____ 4. ver		d. turn
_____ 5. syn-		e. scatter
_____ 6. vert		f. speak
_____ 7. tri-		g. sickness
_____ 8. fid		h. faith
_____ 9. sperse		i. belief
_____10. trans-		j. truth
		k. three
		l. two

B. *Combining context clues and word elements*   Using your knowledge of word elements and context clues, make an intelligent guess at the meaning of the underlined word in each sentence.

11.   The U.S. flag is <u>tricolored</u>.

<u>Tricolored</u> means _____ .

12.   People who could not read or write dictated letters to the <u>scrivener</u>.

<u>Scrivener</u> means _____ .

13.   Thunder and lightning are often <u>concomitant</u> events to rain.

<u>Concomitant</u> means _____ .

14.   The accountant <u>annualized</u> the record-keeping system.

<u>Annualized</u> means _____ .

15.   The bare mountainside was <u>denuded</u> of all trees.

<u>Denuded</u> means _____ .

Definitions

Write the letter of its definition beside each word or figure of speech in the left-hand column. Use each choice only once.

_____ 1. symmetrical   a. at a disadvantage

_____ 2. graphic   b. record of ancestry

_____ 3. pedigree   c. unimportant

_____ 4. destitute   d. referring to financial trust

_____ 5. charisma   e. lack of feeling

_____ 6. retract   f. to destroy

_____ 7. status quo   g. vivid

_____ 8. disparity   h. to hint

_____ 9. trivial   i. to take back

_____ 10. behind the eight ball   j. noticeable

_____ 11. fiduciary   k. existing state of things

_____ 12. apathy   l. a quality that attracts

_____ 13. imply   m. lack of equality

_____ 14. decimate   n. having no money or possessions

_____ 15. bilingual   o. to search thoroughly

     p. balanced

     q. speaking two languages

Words in Context

Write beside each sentence number the letter of the word that best completes that sentence. Use each choice only once.

A. a. metric   e. congregate   i. carte blanche
   b. edict   f. inadvertently   j. veracity
   c. pathology   g. eject   k. biodegradable
   d. creed   h. clichés   l. advocate

_____ 1. The _____ of the desert culture dictated that shelter should be given to any stranger.

_____ 2. I _____ said something stupid.

_____ 3. I am a(n) _____ of the Equal Rights Amendment.

_____ 4. In his speech, the politician made use of so many _____ that he bored everyone.

_____ 5. This _____ material will dissolve into its natural elements within two weeks.

_____ 6. We doubted her _____ because the expression on her face didn't seem honest.

_____ 7. Doctors study the _____ of many diseases.

_____ 8. The large rocket will _____ a small rocket and send it into space.

_____ 9. I wish someone would give me _____ to buy all the new clothes I want.

_____ 10. People often _____ to listen to concerts.

B. a. trilogy   e. intersperse   i. incredulity
    b. colloquial   f. circumspect   j. malady
    c. inaudible   g. adversary   k. gregarious
    d. acrophobia   h. bravado   l. duplicity

_____ 11. The teacher talked to us in _____ language rather than in formal language.

_____ 12. After his _____ was revealed, no one ever trusted him again.

_____ 13. Doctors could not identify the cause of the strange and mysterious _____.

_____ 14. The whisper was _____ to everyone but me.

_____ 15. A champion bowler would be a difficult _____ to beat in a contest.

_____ 16. Because she was a(n) _____ person, she enjoyed getting together with friends.

_____ 17. The _____ man checked to make sure that all of his financial dealings were proper.

_____ 18. I have read only two of the books in the _____.

_____ 19. It is good to _____ your study periods with a few breaks so that you won't get too tired.

_____ 20. The outlaw displayed _____ by making threats that he could not possibly carry out.

ENTIRE BOOK REVIEW EXERCISE

Words to Learn

Definitions   Write the letter of its definition by each word in the left-hand column. Use each choice only once.

A. _____ 1. acrophobia   a. from all parts of the world

_____ 2. invariably   b. to take back

_____ 3. hypocrite   c. necessary

_____ 4. vital   d. carving in stone

_____ 5. cosmopolitan   e. to vary from a path

_____ 6. thrive   f. fear of heights

_____ 7. revoke   g. independent

_____ 8. inscription   h. to gather

_____ 9. symbiotic   i. without change; always

_____ 10. deviate   j. person whose words and actions do not match

                                  k. referring to a dependent relationship

                                  l. to grow and prosper

B. _____ 1. leave no stone unturned   a. bottom point

_____ 2. segregate   b. lacking in luxury

_____ 3. nadir   c. to find guilty

_____ 4. monopoly   d. to investigate financial accounts

_____ 5. perverse   e. contrary to what is good or expected

_____ 6. condemn   f. informal in speech

_____ 7. spartan   g. poor

_____ 8. euphemism   h. to mislead

_____ 9. colloquial   i. exclusive possession or control

_____ 10. audit   j. to separate

                                  k. do everything possible

                                  l. a good term for something unpleasant

Words in context   Write beside each sentence number the letter of the word that best completes that sentence. Use each choice only once.

a. charisma   e. autocratic   i. supplant
b. ambiguous   f. alien   j. contradict
c. circumscribe   g. pandemonium   k. empathy
d. elicit   h. complacent   l. claustrophobia

_____ 1. The senator's _____ caused him to have many followers.

_____ 2. If you _____ the power of the leader too much, he or she will have no power left.

_____ 3. The woman had grown _____ and was certain that she would never be fired, so she rarely worked hard.

_____ 4. As an immigrant, I have _____ for others who have come from foreign lands.

_____ 5. As everyone raced to get the money that had fallen on the floor, _____ broke loose.

_____ 6. My mother became angry when I started to _____ her statements in front of the neighbors.

_____ 7. The man had not yet applied for citizenship, so he was still a(n) _____.

_____ 8. The _____ woman ruled the members of her family.

_____ 9. The movie was so sad that it was able to _____ tears from every member of the audience.

_____ 10. It is not likely that robots will ever _____ human beings.

Learning Strategies

A. *Knowledge*   Write the letter of the choice that best completes each sentence.

_____ 1. The etymology listed as [ME<F<Lat.] shows that the word originally came from _____.

   a. English   b. Middle English   c. French   d. Latin

_____ 2. The abbreviation *tr.v.* is relevant to _____.

   a. the history of a word   b. the meaning of a word   c. the part of speech of a word
   d. nothing

_____ 3. As context clues, such words as *not* and *never* signal a _____.

   a. bad context clue   b. context clue of definition   c. context clue of opposition
   d. context clue of substitution

_____ 4. The word element *mal-* means _____.

   a. many   b. turn   c. bad   d. truth   e. scatter

_____ 5. The word element *dict* means _____.

   a. write   b. say   c. across   d. feeling   e. flock

_____ 6. The word element *tract* means _____.

     a. turn   b. hold   c. belief   d. pull   e. under

_____ 7. The word element *pan-* means _____.

     a. all   b. illness   c. mind   d. out   e. former

_____ 8. The word element *re-* means _____.

     a. not   b. apart   c. back   d. against   e. in

_____ 9. The word element *gen* means _____.

     a. human being   b. birth   c. foot   d. removal from   e. together

_____ 10. The word element *ambi-* means _____.

     a. without   b. twelve   c. year   d. both   e. into

B. *Application* Using word element and context clues, make an intelligent guess at the meaning of the underlined word in each sentence.

11. The doctor examined her <u>vascular</u> system to see if her blood circulation was healthy.

    <u>Vascular</u> means _____ .

12. The <u>cheese-paring</u> husband was never generous, and he made his wife account for every penny that she spent.

    <u>Cheese-paring</u> means _____ .

13. Mary felt <u>disencumbered</u> when someone carried the heavy packages for her.

    <u>Disencumbered</u> means _____ .

14. The <u>monotone</u> chant put us to sleep.

    <u>Monotone</u> means _____ .

15. Some doctors study the <u>pathogenesis</u> of measles.

    <u>Pathogenesis</u> means _____ .

Answer Key to Supplementary Exercises

Multiple-Choice Sentences

Chapter 1, Part 1
1. c 2. b 3. c 4. b 5. c 6. b 7. c 8. a

Chapter 1, Part 2
1. a 2. c 3. b 4. b 5. c 6. c 7. a 8. b

Chapter 2, Part 1
1. c 2. b 3. c 4. a 5. b 6. b 7. a 8. b

Chapter 2, Part 2
1. b 2. c 3. b 4. a 5. c 6. b 7. c 8. a

Chapter 3, Part 1
1. b 2. e 3. c 4. c 5. a 6. a 7. b 8. a

Chapter 3, Part 2
1. a 2. c 3. b 4. b 5. a 6. a 7. c 8. b

Chapter 4, Part 1
1. b 2. c 3. c 4. b 5. c 6. b 7. c 8. b

Chapter 4, Part 2
1. a 2. c 3. b 4. a 5. c 6. b 7. c 8. a

Chapter 5, Part 1
1. c 2. b 3. c 4. b 5. a 6. a 7. c 8. b

Chapter 5, Part 2
1. a 2. c 3. b 4. c 5. b 6. a 7. b 8. b

Chapter 6, Part 1
1. b 2. b 3. a 4. c 5. b 6. b 7. a 8. b

Chapter 6, Part 2
1. b 2. a 3. c 4. c 5. b 6. b 7. c 8. c

Chapter 7, Part 1
1. c 2. b 3. c 4. b 5. b 6. b 7. b 8. c

Chapter 7, Part 2
1. b 2. c 3. b 4. a 5. c 6. c 7. b 8. a

Chapter 8, Part 1
1. c 2. b 3. c 4. b 5. c 6. b 7. c 8. a

Chapter 8, Part 2
1. b 2. c 3. c 4. b 5. c 6. c 7. c 8. a

Chapter 9, Part 1
1. b 2. c 3. c 4. b 5. a 6. a 7. c 8. a

Chapter 9, Part 2
1. b 2. c 3. a 4. c 5. b 6. c 7. a 8. c

Chapter 10, Part 1
1. c 2. c 3. a 4. a 5. b 6. a 7. b 8. b

Chapter 10, Part 2
1. b 2. b 3. c 4. c 5. b 6. a 7. b 8. a

Chapter 11, Part 1
1. c 2. a 3. b 4. c 5. b 6. b 7. b 8. a

Chapter 11, Part 2
1. c 2. b 3. b 4. b 5. c 6. a 7. c 8. c

Chapter 12, Part 1
1. a 2. c 3. c 4. a 5. c 6. c 7. c 8. b

Chapter 12, Part 2
1. c 2. b 3. c 4. a 5. b 6. c 7. c 8. c

Passages

Chapter 1, Part 1
1. Aficionados 2. ascetic 3. adroit
4. altruistic 5. hypocritical 6. gullible
7. disdain 8. capricious 9. intrepid
10. venerable

Chapter 1, Part 2
1. affluent 2. frugal 3. astute 4. amicable
5. alien 6. gauche 7. exuberance 8. novices
9. stoic 10. candid

Chapter 2, Part 1
1. accord 2. diplomacy 3. intervene
4. consumers 5. Entrepreneurs 6. attrition
7. media 8. corroborate 9. catastrophic
10. pacified

Chapter 2, Part 2
1. radically 2. chaotic 3. epitome
4. supplanted 5. apprehend 6. thrive
7. conserve 8. ludicrous 9. reactionary
10. deferred

Chapter 3, Part 1
1. enigmatic 2. clarify 3. emphatically
4. elated 5. concise 6. boisterous 7. thwart
8. skeptical 9. bland 10. confrontation

Chapter 3, Part 2
1. harassing 2. appalled 3. condemned
4. belligerent 5. contended 6. undermine
7. contemplate 8. prohibited 9. flaunt
10. articulated

Chapter 4, Part 1

    1. obsolete   2. augment   3. zeal
    4. jeopardized   5. complacent   6. meticulous
    7. chivalry   8. indulged   9. perpetually
    10. accolades

Chapter 4, Part 2

    1. mammoth   2. cultivation   3. adulated
    4. euphemism   5. withstand   6. successive
    7. mitigate   8. procrastinate   9. accelerate
    10. copious

Chapter 5, Part 1

    1. antithetical   2. equilibrium   3. revelation
    4. equitable   5. reconcile   6. subconscious
    7. antipathy   8. subordinates   9. equivocal
    10. reverted

Chapter 5, Part 2

    1. exorbitant   2. interminably   3. invariably
    4. autonomous   5. eccentricities   6. exploit
    7. ingenious   8. extricate   9. Impartial
    10. incongruous

Chapter 6, Part 1

    1. pseudonym.   2. renown   3. genesis
    4. vivacious   5. congenital   6. misanthropic
    7. viable   8. vitally   9. nominal
    10. philanthropist

Chapter 6, Part 2

    1. pandemonium   2. psyche   3. gargantuan
    4. martial   5. spartan   6. maverick
    7. psychosomatic   8. odyssey   9. chauvinistic
    10. quixotic

Chapter 7, Part 1

    1. deduction   2. tenacious   3. staunch
    4. tenable   5. conducive   6. abstain
    7. dejected   8. abducted   9. status quo
    10. stature

Chapter 7, Part 2

    1. adversary   2. distraught   3. transcend
    4. transitory   5. inadvertently   6. perverse
    7. retract   8. circumspect   9. circumvent
    10. transform

Chapter 8, Part 1

    1. contemporary   2. compatible   3. discord
    4. concur   5. disparity   6. disreputable
    7. synopsize   8. coherent   9. collaborated
    10. synthesis

Chapter 8, Part 2

    1. congregations   2. charismatic   3. zenith
    4. nadir   5. bravado   6. gregarious
    7. interspersed   8. cuisines   9. sparsity
    10. dispersed

Chapter 9, Part 1

    1. decade   2. monopoly   3. unilateral
    4. unanimity   5. dilemma   6. bipartisan
    7. bilingual   8. trivial   9. decimate
    10. duplicity

Chapter 9, Part 2

    1. annals   2. perennial   3. ambivalent
    4. ambiguous   5. integrity   6. disintegrated
    7. centennial   8. magnitude   9. magnanimous
    10. metric

Chapter 10, Part 1

    1. veracity   2. verify   3. fidelity
    4. incredulous   5. fiduciary   6. credibility
    7. creeds   8. defiant   9. claustrophobic
    10. veritable

Chapter 10, Part 2

    1. star-crossed   2. deviated   3. gave carte
blanche   4. behind the eight ball   5. left no
stone unturned   6. delude   7. nonchalant
    8. destitute   9. held out an olive branch
    10. tongue-in-cheek

Chapter 11, Part 1

    1. conspicuous   2. pedigrees   3. impeded
    4. inaudible   5. pathetic   6. pathology
    7. auditory   8. expedite   9. introspection
    10. auspicious

Chapter 11, Part 2

    1. malpractice   2. malady   3. beneficial
    4. apathetic   5. malevolence   6. anonymous
    7. anarchy   8. biopsy   9. benign
    10. Benefactors

Chapter 12, Part 1

    1. dictators   2. edicts   3. revoke
    4. monologue   5. ecology   6. invoke
    7. advocate   8. Contradicting   9. vociferate
    10. prologue

Chapter 12, Part 2

    1. transcribed   2. manuscript   3. affected
    4. graphic   5. inscriptions   6. implies
    7. effect   8. demographic   9. conscious
    10. infer

Review Exercises

Chapters 1 Through 6

Learning Strategies 1. c 2. c 3. b 4. keep trying 5. height; best 6. impatient; restless 7. ringing; pealing 8. wild; animal-like 9. violations 10. careless 11. make more lifelike 12. acquitted; freed from blame 13. living again after death 14. mental illness 15. part of a portion

Word Element Meanings 1. f 2. a 3. g 4. c 5. d

Definitions 1. f 2. q 3. h 4. c 5. p 6. a 7. g 8. e 9. n 10. d 11. m 12. k 13. o 14. b 15. j

Words in Context A. 1. l—martial 2. h—adroit 3. d—stoic 4. k—enigma 5. g—capricious 6. c—exploit 7. b—viable 8. j—mitigating 9. f—antidote 10. a—accord B. 11. a—boycott 12. c—appall 13. i—obsolete 14. b—extricate 15. h—liberal 16. k—impartial 17. l—genocide 18. e—subdue 19. j—emulate 20. f—fraternal

Chapters 7 Through 12

Learning Strategies 1. l 2. f 3. a 4. j 5. c 6. d 7. k 8. h 9. e 10. b 11. three-colored 12. person who wrote letters 13. occurring at the same time 14. put on a yearly basis 15. stripped; made bare

Definitions 1. p 2. g 3. b 4. n 5. l 6. i 7. k 8. m 9. c 10. a 11. d 12. e 13. h 14. f 15. q

Words in Context A. 1. d—creed 2. f—inadvertently 3. l—advocate 4. h—clichés 5. k—biodegradable 6. j—veracity 7. c—pathology 8. g—eject 9. i—carte blanche 10. e—congregate B. 11. b—colloquial 12. l—duplicity 13. j—malady 14. c—inaudible 15. g—adversary 16. k—gregarious 17. f—circumspect 18. a—trilogy 19. e—intersperse 20. h—bravado

Entire Book

Words to Learn: Definitions A. 1. f 2. i 3. j 4. c 5. a 6. l 7. b 8. d 9. k 10. e B. 1. k 2. j 3. a 4. i 5. e 6. c 7. b 8. l 9. f 10. d

Words in Context 1. a—charisma 2. c—circumscribe 3. h—complacent 4. k—empathy 5. g—pandemonium 6. j—contradict 7. f—alien 8. e—autocratic 9. d—elicit 10. i—supplant

Learning Strategies 1. d 2. c 3. c 4. c 5. b 6. d 7. a 8. c 9. b 10. d 11. referring to the circulation of blood 12. stingy 13. having a burden taken away; freed 14. having one note 15. origin of disease